FREEDOM FROM THE BOTTLE

*A Guide to Recovery for alcoholics,
their partners and children*

LIZ CUTLAND

Foreword by Anthony Hopkins

GATEWAY BOOKS, BATH

Also by the author:
KICK HEROIN

First published in 1990
by Gateway Books,
The Hollies, Wellow,
Bath BA2 8QJ

©1990 Liz Cutland

Cover design by Studio B, Bristol
Set in 10 on 12 Plantin by
Photosetting and Secretarial Services of Yeovil
Printed and bound by
Billings of Worcester

British Library Cataloguing in Publication Data
Cutland, Liz, 1947—
    Freedom from the bottle : a guide to recovery for
alcoholics, their partners and children.
    1. Alcoholics. Treatment
    I. Title
    362.2'9286

ISBN 0-946551-55-3

Cover photo: detail from CHE 18114 –   *J Haier (1816–91)*
Monks in a Cellar, 1873
Cheltenham Art Gallery
and Museums, Glos./
Bridgeman Art Library,
London

Contents

Foreword

I drank for fifteen years. I was always a troubled drinker — morose and depressed, with a very low tolerance for alcohol. No matter what my preference of the moment — beer, wine, whisky, vodka, gin, tequila, brandy — it all went to my brain the same way; rapidly, effectively and disastrously.

There were some happy times in the early days. I always enjoyed the initial effects of that first drink — the loosening of inhibitions and anxieties. My problem was that I couldn't get loosened enough! I wasn't able to relax sufficiently to enjoy drinking in what is called a civilized manner. I was a sloppy drinker, a guzzler and a gulper. I drank fast, ate fast, did everything fast, as if driven by some irrational fear that there would never be enough to go around, or that I would be cheated of some ultimate pleasure. Even now, after almost fourteen years without a drink, I find it pretty well impossible to understand those feelings.

I suspect that the root of alcoholism, or any other form of addiction or personality disorder, can be traced back into very early development. That is only an opinion. It is not an excuse, nor is it a justification for the havoc that alcoholism causes. All I know is that most alcoholics I meet, whether they are sober or still drinking, identify with that strange feeling of un-ease with themselves and the world.

Although raised as an only child in an ordinary family, doted upon, and sometimes worried over — but no more, no less than in any other family — I felt from early days an overwhelming anxiety that I would be deprived of something that was rightly mine. Just what that 'something' was is hard to define, but fear became the driving force in my life for the next thirty years. Every human being experiences these feelings, so there was nothing unique about my condition. What seemed to be at fault, however, was my reaction to reality and my inability to respond to events or to my emotions in a 'mature' way. Everything was a drama or a cause for deep concern. Perhaps that is why I became an actor!

Eventually the inevitable happened — my first encounter with that elixir of life — BOOZE! I'd found the answer! Instant gratification and immediate release from fear and self-doubt. At last I felt whole and at one with the human race. Ah! those fleeting moments of euphoria and intoxication were pure gold. I was ten feet tall and had the world by the tail! But they were fleeting moments — brief interludes in the tumult of my increasing fears and nagging self doubts. Within a very short time my pleasurable drinking was giving way to violent mood swings. These were later to be followed by oblivion and blackout drinking.

Although I had started out as a reasonably moderate drinker — the usual gatherings in pubs, friendly conversation, etc. — I soon became a daily drinker. It had just become a habit and a way of life. All pretty harmless stuff. All actors drank, or so I thought. This was what separated the men from the boys. It was all such chauvinistic, elitist claptrap! Those actors who didn't drink, or had the occasional half pint of beer, just to be friendly, were beneath my contempt. They were, in my expert opinion, probably very untalented, certainly dull, dead from the neck up and not worth more than a minute of my consideration or condescension. What arrogance! Secretly though, deep, deep down inside, I envied them. They puzzled me. They seemed to be content with their lives. They didn't get stirred up about things the way I did. I regarded them as a different species of human being. In my heart I envied and resented them. And so I drank more and more to quench my unquenchable thirst. In other areas of my life, too, I became insatiable. I forced myself to work harder and longer than anyone else, demanding more of myself and of others — working colleagues, family and what few friends I had. I worked harder and more fanatically in order to outsmart, outwit and outmanoeuvre everyone else. No one was going to rumble me!

And when professional success came, I lived in fear that that success would be taken away or that someone else would be even more successful than me. I spent those years constantly looking over my shoulder. It all seems pretty laughable and pathetic now, looking back, but at the time I felt I was in hell. His Majesty the Monstrous Baby now reigned supreme inside me, waving his rattle and banging his spoon, demanding yet more and more gratification and, in turn, more alcohol to dampen the fire. I was in the squirrel cage chasing my own tail.

On the outside I probably looked all right. But those who were close to me sensed that all was not too well. I was committing suicide on the instalment plan because life was not living up to my expectations and was disappointing me deeply, and so I would revenge myself upon the world by inviting oblivion into my brain, in an orgy of rage and self-pity.

But I was not alone (although I didn't recognise this at the time). There were many thousands like me, caught in the same trap, because alcoholism comes in many cunning and subtle disguises. This is not to say that everyone who goes to the pub or likes to drink is an alcoholic — on the contrary. There are millions of people who can drink, but who have a natural ability to control or moderate their drinking. Many once in a while get drunk or celebrate and have just one over the top, but next day return to normal and get on with their lives. They can take it or leave it. To them drink is no big deal!

In 1974 I travelled to America pursuing the Goddess of Fame and Fortune and arrived in New York to take on the world. I was in a very successful play and I too was riding the crest of a wave. The sweet smell of success! All my ambitions and dreams were coming true. I had made myself and my wife so many well-meant promises: "When I get 'there'", I once told her, "then I'll shape up and get my life in order". Well, I got 'there', wherever 'there' is — I'd 'made it'; and then for some puzzling reason all hell broke loose. I was in the grip of full-blown alcoholism. I had a tiger, not the world, by the tail. I remember sitting on the corner of the bed one night and saying to my wife that I didn't know what was happening to me, "I think I'm going insane, I can't stop drinking".

My time was running out until finally, one day in Los Angeles, I was forced to concede total defeat. I threw in the towel and phoned a self-help encounter group. That moment changed my life. It happened at the end of December 1975; it was the only worthwhile action that I've taken in my life and for some miraculous reason I have not wanted or taken a drink of alcohol since then. My life has been transformed.

I was asked to write an introduction to this excellent book and for some time hesitated and cogitated because I feel that I cannot take one particle of credit for what has happened to me. A gift was handed me on a plate and I am now a sober, recovering alcoholic. There is no cure for alcoholism, but there is a solution and I live with that solution now, but I could never have done it on my own. I needed help and that moment of asking for help finally broke through my sick and distorted ego and I was set free from the nightmare: the monkey was off my back. I feel so grateful but I know that there are many, many thousands of people who are utterly baffled by their inability to control their drinking. If this book helps just a few onto the road to sanity and back into life then it will be a triumph.

Anthony Hopkins

To Peg and John, with love

Acknowledgements

I greatly appreciate Anthony Hopkins' generosity in writing the Foreword, and would like to thank him for sharing in such a personal way.

My grateful thanks to Alison who patiently typed and retyped the original pages of this book; to Jessie who has her own special knowledge and who took time to read the manuscript, giving me her constructive and honest opinions; to my colleagues at Broadway Lodge and Farm Place who supported me as these pages became a reality; to Alick Bartholomew for his great patience and faith in publishing this book. Above all, to all my friends who shared their experiences of alcoholism with me. It was their openness and truthfulness of those recovering alcoholics and their families which made it possible for me to write this book. Every case described here is real. Only the names have been changed — for obvious reasons. Each person mentioned showed their own unique struggle to find Freedom from the Bottle. In turn, I hope this book will help others find that path to recovery.

Introduction

Who Needs Freedom?

Alcoholism is one of the major killing diseases of this century. Yet, so many people desperately seeking recovery for themselves or a loved one, are often thwarted in their efforts to find successful treatment. This is because alcoholism is also one of the most misunderstood illnesses in our culture; it is enmeshed and hidden in a web of denial, mystique, myths, fear, embarrassment and ignorance. In fact, as with those people who suffered tuberculosis and cancer in previous eras, we often stigmatise those who are alcoholic and look the other way. I am delighted for my friends who are drug addicts that the media have created a fuss about the extent of their problem. At the same time, I am saddened because I am aware that the problem of alcoholism is much more widespread and just as fatal. Yet, it is still very successfully swept under the carpet and often ignored.

These pages have really niggled their way into existence because of my own sense of frustration. I started to work with alcoholics and their families in 1975. The knowledge and experience that I have gained has given me an insight that many people, given the right opportunity, indeed do recover from this traumatic illness. Yet, at the same time, I know that many people who become alcoholic slip through the medical and social nets and die horrible, premature deaths. This happens so often because our society is uninformed, shrugs its shoulders apathetically or buries its head in the sand. There is not nearly enough being done to help. Each day alcoholic fatalities occur as a result of drinking and driving accidents; from heart or liver diseases resulting from the organs having to cope with too much alcohol over a period of time; from being asphyxiated by one's own vomit; from fire caused by smoking cigarettes while drunk, or being too far gone to remember leaving something boiling on the cooker. Most of these deaths might have been prevented if there was a greater awareness and understanding of the disease of alcoholism.

Despite the slow but continuing growth of information in the media about alcoholism, there are still a number of myths and assumptions made about people who become dependent on alcohol. For example, the stereotype of an alcoholic still tends to be that of a loner; a dirty old man in a mac tied together with string, sleeping under the arches, wrapped in a newspaper and clutching a bottle of cheap red wine. As a result, we tend to deny that this illness can happen in our family. We are blind to the fact that alcoholism is no respecter of class, culture or creed. We forget that some priests, doctors, housewives, company directors, airline pilots, train-drivers, politicians, schoolboys, hairdressers, senior citizens, (to name but a few) are actively suffering from the disease.

Consequently, I do not plan that this book should spend time moralizing about moderating one's consumption of alcohol; fight the advertising campaigns which influence the young and easily persuaded; or try to alter the licensing laws. Indeed, prevention of further development of alcoholism is a very important issue. However, I have no power to change these things and many people are already involved in shouting from those particular bandwagons. Instead, this book is an attempt to face the reality of the existing problem of alcoholism and an effort to reach some of the estimated 1,000,000 people in the United Kingdom who are believed to suffer from chronic alcohol problems, and the even larger number who are on their way along that devastating path of addiction to alcohol.

In the first chapters, I will attempt to describe what alcoholism is. One of the problems that causes a great deal of confusion in the field of treating this disorder is the perplexity and indecisiveness of the medical and social work professions. Like some of the public at large, many regard addiction to alcohol as a moral weakness and wish alcoholics would 'pull themselves together'. Alcoholism is a very unromantic illness. The drinking alcoholic does not endear himself to any busy person; he causes havoc in the casualty department, he demands a lot of precious time, he continues to drink after many caring souls have spent much time trying to help him. His illness cannot be cut out by the surgeon's knife. Traditional psychiatric methods of putting the main emphasis of treatment on looking for the underlying symptoms prove futile in the vast majority of cases. Doctors, psychiatrists, nurses, social workers, probation officers have probably had only a few hours of their lengthy training studying this, one of the main killer diseases of this century. In their discomfort they fall into the trap of playing with semantics. Some people decide that the label 'alcoholic' is destructive or rude, and new, less threatening terms like 'alcoholic dependence syndrome' and 'problem drinker' are introduced. Eminent physicians argue about controlled drinking programmes versus total abstinence. For members of the public who are already distraught, frightened and desperate for help, it only adds to the sense of futility and frustration.

I hope that this book will cut through a lot of this clutter. I strongly believe that if the subject of alcoholism was kept simple and the goals of recovery made clear and specific, then many more people could have the opportunity to get well. Sadly, at this time, too many people in the helping professions are either too busy or too uninterested to learn more about the alcoholic, his illness and recovery.

This book is based on the school of thought that alcoholics, once they have crossed the thin line from heavy social drinker, can never go back to controlled drinking. I do believe that there are some drinkers who, during periods of stress, may have some problems with their drinking. However, if they can resume a limited, moderate, responsible and controlled consumption of alcohol continued over a period of several months — then by my definition, they are not alcoholic. 'Going on the Wagon' is much easier for an alcoholic to handle than light, controlled drinking. Most irrational drinking causes problems of one sort or another for the person involved. Nevertheless, the heavy social drinker usually realises his situation and can control it. He learns quite quickly from his painful experience with alcohol and modifies the amount. Even though an alcoholic has been in trouble on numerous occasions over drinking, he still continues to drink, blind to the fact that that is what is causing his problems.

I hope that some of those people who are fearful of where their drinking is taking them, will obtain some relief and help from reading these pages. However, the other groups of people at whom I am aiming this book are those who have a close relationship with someone who is alcoholic; those who are despairing because they believe, and may even have been told, that their addicted drinker is beyond help; those who have been wrongly encouraged to believe that the dependence on alcohol is somehow their fault; those who have become isolated because of the fear, secrecy and pessimism that surrounds the disease; and those who are frantically doing their best to try and control or stop a loved one's drinking, but are being pulled down into the depths of despair as each attempt fails. My goal is to provide those readers who fall into any of the above categories with some hope, clarification, relief, understanding of the illness and its consequences, as well as constructive advice on how to help themselves and their alcoholic sufferer.

There are several chapters in this book devoted to illustrating how the family network has been affected by alcoholism. They also describe how, through ignorance, but the best of intentions, the individuals involved may have colluded in an unacknowledged conspiracy of silence and enabled the suffering alcoholic further into the illness. For every alcohol-dependent person there are, on average, three other people enduring a great deal of stress in trying to cope with the chaos that results from the illness. In order to help an alcoholic find recovery, families will discover that they have to change their attitudes and behaviour towards the sufferer. Alcoholism is no one's fault. No one causes it. However, many alcoholics are pushed further into the disease by their families and other close relationships. Helping an alcoholic means learning to love in a different way: detaching and letting the alcoholic be responsible for himself (see chapter 5).

One of the most important factors that I hope will come across clearly is that alcoholics are not the only casualties who suffer as a result of this disease. My experience has shown me that people in a close relationship with an alcoholic endure more pain than he does. They live with the raw agony and isolation, knowing that it is not only the alcoholic who is stigmatised, but also the family with whom he is involved. They know that the outrageous behaviour of the alcoholic is often very public and they are aware that uninformed people will point the finger and blame. The alcoholic is often anaesthetized and unaware of, or insensitive to, other people's reactions. Those people close to the alcoholic are very much in touch with that profound feeling of shame. In their own minds, they are failures as human beings because they have not been able to control the alcoholic's drinking. Worse still, they often believe they have caused the dependence on alcohol. They stay because they believe it is their duty to help the drinker. Actually, some families need to leave for the sake of their own sanity. It takes a lot of courage to do so.

It is not only the adults who have to endure the stress. The children who grow up in such a family are expected to cope with the violence, the chaos, the fear, the tension, the never knowing what to expect next, the lack of parental support. They look at other families and know that theirs is different. Children in alcoholic homes are often forgotten. Forgotten by parents (drinking and non-drinking); forgotten by professionals helping alcoholics; forgotten by their friends, because many children of alcoholics become withdrawn and isolated; forgotten by their brothers and sisters because they are just too busy surviving. Many have been abused by their drinking parent, physically or sexually. The non-addicted parent can also become violent as a result of living with the stress of alcoholism. At best, the young people have learned to survive the best way they know how, usually by suppressing their needs and feelings. In many cases, they have learned that neither parent is there for emotional support. The alcoholic is too involved in his drinking; the non-addicted parent too preoccupied with the chaos caused by the drinker.

There is not enough done to reach and help the alcoholics in this country — even less done to help their spouses or partners. Sadly, the amount of understanding and support given to the children is almost non-existent. Children of alcoholics are the next link in the destructive chain that has already stretched over generations. A very high proportion become addicted to alcohol or drugs themselves. Others marry, or become involved in a series of relationships with other addicted people. This is the only kind of relationship they know how to cope with. Looking after addicts is how they have learned to feel like worthwhile people. However, as I've described later in the book, that caretaking behaviour helps to perpetuate the progression of the disease of alcoholism.

As far as I am aware, few programmes designed to prevent alcohol abuse address the high probability that children of alcoholics will carry their involvement with this illness into the next adult generation. I do hope this book helps make others aware of this danger, resulting in some young victims finding the help and support they need.

At the back of the book I have listed a number of self-help groups who will help alcoholics and their families to recover. Since its foundation in 1935, Alcoholics Anonymous has been the most successful programme for helping alcoholics. It is a voluntary organisation with a network of meetings taking place all over this country and in other parts of the world. No professional organisation has achieved the same degree of success in helping those addicted to alcohol as has this body. Its sister organisation, Al-Anon, also a self-help group, helps friends or relatives of alcoholics. Like Farm Place and similar professionally-run treatment centres, it believes that family members need and deserve as much help as the dependent person. There is also support provided for young people in similar groups called Adult Children of Alcoholics and Alateen.

Fourteen years ago, because of my lack of knowledge, I dismissed alcoholics as hopeless, helpless people who had a desire for self-destruction. Initially, I had no ambition to work with addicted people or their families, but one of the reasons I have stayed in this field is the tremendous satisfaction I get from seeing the alcoholics and the family members recover and find new and meaningful ways of life.

Alcoholism affects both sexes. Where appropriate I have illustrated examples where the woman is an alcoholic. However, to keep the text uncomplicated and easy to read, I have described the alcoholic as 'he'. I have no intention of being sexist and I have tried to come up with a solution which gives attention to both men and women. Also, I use the term 'family' a lot in this book. By that I mean any individual, group or network of people who have a close relationship with an alcoholic.

The method described in this book is one way that an alcoholic and his surrounding family can become well, find peace of mind and the freedom to live their lives as they choose.

If this text achieves nothing else, I hope it convinces some people that there is a way out; that the pain and misery will go if you are prepared to learn about alcoholism and the role of the family, and work at changing your attitudes; that it is not a pointless exercise setting your goals for recovery — that there is hope.

Part I

The Alcoholic and Alcoholism

1

What is Alcoholism?

"Alcoholism is a progressive illness. We go through the three stages of social drinking, trouble drinking and merry-go-round drinking. We land in hospitals and jails. We eventually lose our homes, our families and our self-respect. Yes, alcoholism is a progressive illness and there are only three ends to it — the insane asylum, the morgue or total abstinence."

Twenty-four hours a day

Mary is 44 years old. Four years ago she returned to teaching after her three children all became teenagers. David, her ex-husband, is a well respected dentist.

Although Mary had a reputation for being the life and soul of various parties some years ago, at that time she had not drunk alcohol for a period of about five years. Her friends and neighbours understood why she did not drink. They were relieved that the incident had not happened to them. After all, most of them had been at that neighbourhood sherry party and most of them had had a couple of drinks. What no one knew (except Mary) was that as on other days, she had had a few drinks at lunchtime when she was on her own. If her friends had known that, perhaps another mum would have volunteered not to drink and pick the children up from school. Fortunately, no one had died as a result of the car accident, but it had been touch and go for her eight year old daughter. She had been in hospital for some time with serious injuries.

It was getting near to Christmas. Mary had been feeling miserable recently. She had been to see her doctor and he had prescribed a course of tranquillizers, encouraging her to find more interests in life. The effect of the tranquillizers seemed to be wearing off. On about three occasions when she was feeling really down, she took one tablet more than had been prescribed. Nevertheless, Mary decided that she would make this a special Christmas for those dear to her. Christmas would be a family day and she had invited a number of friends round on Boxing Day for a get-together. As it was a special occasion, she thought she might allow herself to have a couple of drinks on both those days. She had not had one of those terrible cravings for a drink for some time now.

She discussed this with her husband, David. A few years ago he had been really concerned about the amount of alcohol she had been getting through and even more concerned about the way she seemed to change her personality when she drank. At parties, everyone thought she was witty, fun to be with, slightly on the wild side. At home, she was argumentative and on a couple of occasions, quite violent. She seemed to lose interest in the home and the family. After the accident, with the anxiety over their daughter's health, the loss of her driving licence, the embarrassment and avoidance of friends, David had found it very difficult to forgive her. However, he had been quite proud of the way she had pulled herself together over the last few years. She obviously had got the problem licked — whatever it was. He agreed quite happily that she should have two glasses of wine on both Christmas and Boxing Day.

In fact, the Christmas holiday was a great success. Friends and family were full of praise for Mary's efforts and were pleased to see that she had relaxed enough to have a small amount of alcohol. Previously Mary had been feeling guilty that her not-drinking had inhibited David and prevented him from enjoying a bottle of wine at weekends. Now she felt more confident that she could handle alcohol, she suggested they might share a bottle of wine with Sunday lunch. David thought this was a marvellous idea. For about six weeks this pattern continued. Mary was feeling better than she had for a long time. She was sticking to the prescribed amount of tranquillizers.

Her best friend invited her and David to make up a foursome at a dinner party. Although Mary had planned only to have a couple of drinks, everyone else was drinking quite freely and she decided she would join in the party spirit. Mary had a lovely time that evening. She had drunk much more than she intended to and had been able to avoid David's anxious looks. However, she hadn't felt so free or had so much fun for a long time. Within a short period of time, Mary was drinking most evenings of the week.

One Saturday, Mary had a heated argument with her fifteen-year-old daughter. She was so upset and agitated afterwards that she went to the medicine cabinet to find her tranquillizers. Unfortunately, she had run out because she had started to increase the daily prescribed dosage. She told the family she was going to do the family shopping. In fact, she went straight to the drinks counter, bought a half bottle of vodka, put it in her handbag, drove home, sat in the shed at the bottom of the garden and drank a large part of it. On Monday, Mary went to see her doctor and renewed her prescription for her tranquillizers. She hated to be without them.

Mary was dependent on both alcohol and tranquillizers. In fact, she had lost control again. She was obsessed with finding that lovely, intoxicating feeling.

I met Mary three years after this time. She was in a treatment centre for alcoholism. During that period, her husband had left her. He later told her it was because of her drinking. He was tired of the lies, deceit, and aggression, never knowing what to expect next. He became involved with another lady.

Another drinking crisis that eventually brought her into treatment was the possibility that she might lose her job. She had once been an excellent teacher. Now she was no longer able to concentrate properly. She had had a lot of absences from work and parents had started to complain about her ineffectiveness. Her headmaster, who had been very supportive all through the period of her divorce, had recently confronted her with smelling of alcohol fairly early in the morning. His brother happened to be a member of Alcoholics Anonymous, a recovering alcoholic, and he was able to recommend where she could get some help.

Although the problem of alcoholism had been developing in Mary's life for at least ten to twelve years, it had progressed, unacknowledged, until her headmaster's confrontation. Everyone else thought all Mary had to do was 'pull herself together'. No one had enough knowledge of the early symptoms of alcoholism to intervene. Several tragedies had to happen first. Actually, Mary was more fortunate than most. Someone in her life had the knowledge and courage to suggest that she might have a problem with alcohol and also pointed her in the right direction to get help. As a result of her boss's intervention, her illness was arrested. So many people suffering in the same way are ignored or shunned and left to progress into the late, chronic stages of this illness.

I have used the example of Mary to illustrate some of the main characteristics of alcoholism; the subtle insidiousness of the onset of the illness. In this chapter, I will attempt to highlight some of these features and share much of the information I have learned over the years.

Alcoholism is Cunning, Baffling and Powerful

Alcoholism is a monster which devours many good and talented people. Nobody knows all about it; even to the experts some aspects of it remain a mystery. This disease fascinates, puzzles, repels and frustrates many people. We have looked for reasons, tried to understand it scientifically, attempted to fix it within psychiatric and medical models of treatment, often in vain. We have tried to find logical answers for our unanswered questions. Yet, despite years of hard work and research, the answers continue to elude and baffle us.

I do not claim to fully understand what alcoholism is, although I have worked with alcoholics and their families in a full-time capacity since 1975. I do know that it is devastating in its effects: on the individual, on the family, on industry, on our legal systems, on our society as a whole. It is a much more widespread addiction than the much publicised street drug problems. Also I am aware that many people are frightened of it and pretend that it does not exist or that it is something else. Many people are so because they do not know what to do.

I hope that these pages will help open some people's minds to what alcoholism is: a disease that is treatable. One that need not shorten one's life expectancy if the right help is found.

The main characteristics of alcoholism can be described under the following sixteen headings:

Alcoholism is a Disease

The whole of this book, and the treatment philosophy which I adhere to, is based on an assumption. These days I take it for granted that alcoholism is a disease in its own right — not just an underlying symptom of some deep emotional problem. I believe in the disease concept of alcoholism for two reasons:

1. When it is treated as such, I have seen so many people recover and find a quality of life that many non-alcoholics never achieve.

2. Over the last decade and more, I have worked with thousands of alcoholics from all sorts of backgrounds and personalities. I continue to be amazed at the similarity and repetitiveness of the pattern of symptoms of alcoholism in each individual. Some of those symptoms are described at the end of this chapter.

I have to admit that I am somewhat of a cynic by nature. It took me well over a year of working in this field to be convinced that it is an illness and not just a behavioural problem. I expect that a lot of readers will have the same problem. Others may find some relief in identifying with the characteristics of the disease, described in this chapter.

Like other major illnesses such as cancer or meningitis, despite the thousands of pounds spent on research, we do not fully comprehend what causes it, what makes one person become an alcoholic, while the majority of drinkers do not. It seems that there is increasingly more evidence to support the belief in a genetic predisposition. Apparently, some specialists and researchers believe that potential alcoholics have a different biochemical reaction to alcohol in the brain. However, this research is not yet conclusive.

I do know that an alcoholic is more likely to recover from this illness if, in fact, he can accept that he is a sick person who can get well, rather than how others usually view him, as a bad or morally weak person who needs to become good.

Alcoholism is a Permanent, Progressive and Terminal Illness

Alcoholism gets worse if it is not arrested. Sometimes an alcoholic drinker will hit a plateau, or a period of remission, when the drinking behaviour appears to stay constant for months or even years. However, over a period of time it is inevitable that the disease will progress towards more and more serious deterioration. The worsening of the condition will affect the physical, mental and spiritual components of the sufferer. It is often said that alcoholics need to hit 'rock bottom' before they can be successfully treated. This is not so. The earlier the treatment, the more chances there are for it to succeed. If the disease is not arrested then the inevitable outcome is the death of the alcoholic.

Once an alcoholic, he or she is always an alcoholic. This does not mean that the individual always has to drink or behave alcoholically. He can learn to live a normal life as long as he abstains from drinking alcohol. Nevertheless, it is important to be aware that the disease appears to progress, even though the alcoholic has not been drinking for a long period of time. There are many reports of alcoholics who have resumed drinking after periods of abstinence of 5, 10, 15 or more years. Those close to that person often state that the deterioration in the alcoholic's behaviour is quick and obvious. It has got worse, not better, after a long period of not drinking.

Alcoholism is an Often Ignored Disease

While observing a drinker suffering from jaundice caused by alcohol-related liver disease, or withdrawal shakes or hallucinations, I believe that most people would have no doubt that the sufferer was ill. Also, I think that several people by this point would be willing to believe that the illness was probably caused by prolonged dependence on alcohol. They might even be prepared to use that most shunned word 'alcoholism' to describe the symptoms observed. Indeed at this crucial stage, many would accept the need for the affected person to abstain from alcohol use.

Sadly, by the time a drinker reaches these serious physical conditions, he is in the late, advanced stages of a fatal disease: an illness that for years has been slowly and insidiously progressing unrecognised or unacknowledged by the alcoholic himself, the medical profession and other people in our society — including his close relatives. An illness that has wreaked havoc within his family, his friendships, his job, with his finances as well as his health.

Professionals may have been consulted by the drinker or his family. However, because of the denial of the drinker, inadequate training of the professionals and a strong cultural bias against considering a person alcoholic until the late stages of the illness, the help has been minimal and inappropriate. Doctors may have made suggestions about cutting down on alcohol consumption while prescribing some tranquillizers which are just as harmful to alcoholics as whisky or gin. Social workers or marriage guidance counsellors may have suggested ways of improving marital communication, ignoring the fact that drinking is causing the major problem in the relationship.

It is a fact that many alcoholics die before they reach these final stages. They die from car accidents caused by drunken driving; from a broken neck after falling down the stairs while intoxicated; from accidentally overdosing on a combination of alcohol and other drugs; from setting fire to themselves while smoking and drinking. They die from a heart condition or bleeding ulcer which has been agitated by drinking alcohol. *They die because everyone has been waiting for the final stages of the illness to reveal themselves before they are prepared to acknowledge that the real problem is alcoholism. It is one of the most ignored addictions in our culture.*

Alcoholism is a Drug Addiction

Before we go any further in considering what alcoholism is, I believe it is important that we look at how we, as a society, use alcohol.

For most people, drinking is a generally harmless activity which is an important part of our socialising ritual. When we celebrate a marriage, a birthday, a christening, a business transaction, we frequently use alcohol to toast the event. To most individuals alcohol is something to be enjoyed, occasionally alone, but more often with friends and family. For many, alcohol is an interesting, pleasurable part of life — but not essential. Social drinkers rarely drink beyond the achievement of mild relaxation.

At times, some may use alcohol as a tranquillizer. It may be used to help you relax after a hard day's work; it may be drunk to give you 'Dutch courage' in a social situation or to help deal with upset feelings. Others imbibe to cheer themselves up. When it is taken for such reasons it is being used like a medicine, a sedative; taken to relieve stress or make one feel better. Again, for many, it is a fairly harmless activity which occasionally happens and often other constructive ways are found to improve one's feelings of well-being.

However, for about 8 – 10% of those who drink, alcohol use slowly shifts from a harmless to a damaging activity. There is a very thin line between stress-relief drinking and alcoholism. For these people, the need for that medicine gradually moves to needing it to relax before going to parties; needing it to make love to one's partner; to sleep at night; to wake up in the morning; to get through the day; to anaesthetize any emotional pain; in fact, needing it because that terrible, powerful urge is saying so.

Alcoholism is a Physical Addiction

Like the other chemicals that some people use to make them feel better, alcohol is an addictive substance. Some people become as physically and emotionally dependent on it as others do to prescribed tranquillizers, heroin, amphetamine, cocaine and barbiturates. In fact, once a person has become physically dependent on alcohol, the withdrawal symptoms when he stops drinking can be dangerous — more dangerous than coming off the other drugs like heroin, amphetamine (speed) or cocaine. If someone has been drinking heavily and regularly for a long time and wants to stop, he should have medical supervision. If he does not do so he could experience the D.T.s (delirium tremens), the name given to violent withdrawal tremors which are sometimes accompanied by seeing or hearing things that are not there. Withdrawal fits can follow. If these fits are not dealt with under medical care, they can be fatal. I am not medically trained. Other books can deal with this section more professionally and knowledgeably than I can (I would recommend *Coming off Drink* by Ditzler & Ditzler). It is inevitable that as the alcoholic progresses into the chronic stages he is in danger of damaging his liver, his stomach, his heart, his brain and other vital parts of his anatomy.

Alcoholism is a Chemical Dependence

The treatment centre where I work successfully treats alcoholics, heroin addicts and also some of those dependent on tranquillizers under the same roof, using the same method of treatment. We do this because we are of the opinion that all of these dependencies are, in fact, the same illness. The professional jargon, or collective term, used to describe this disease is *Chemical Dependence.*

The first reaction of many alcoholics and their relatives is to be horrified that they are being equated with 'junkies' who use illegal drugs and those who have become hooked on prescribed drugs such as tranquillizers. However, these days it is becoming rare to find an alcoholic who is just dependent on alcohol. Many who have been introduced to such drugs as heminevrin, or sleeping pills, by the medical profession, find that they produce a similar sensation to alcohol. Usually, alcoholics do not use drugs as prescribed, needing more and more to produce the required effect, or mixing them with alcohol to get a quicker 'high'. Several young alcoholics will experiment with street drugs such as marijuana, heroin or cocaine and substitute one for the other. The feeling that comes from the chemical is the most important thing to an alcoholic. Where it comes from is secondary. For many, alcohol is probably the favourite drug, but other medicines which change the mood are liked too. Cough medications which contain alcohol or codeine are popular with some alcoholics for this reason. For some, in the later stages of the illness, any substance which contains alcohol will do; even chemicals such as aftershave and methylated spirits.

Alcoholism is an Overwhelming Compulsion to Drink

I have to admit that there is nothing new or original in what I am sharing in these pages. Everything that I mention here has been taught me. My information comes from my experience of working with many alcoholics and their families. Also, I was trained as a counsellor by people who have been recovering from this illness for several years. Currently, a number of my colleagues are recovering alcoholics. I mention this because it has taken a great deal of patience on their parts to help me, a non-alcoholic, to understand the urge or loss of control that happens to a person who has this illness. Even now, I do not understand it fully because I have not experienced it. However, as a result of my friends' help, I believe I understand this illness well enough to be reasonably effective in my field of work. Unfortunately, many people who want to help alcoholics or other addicts, have not taken the time or been given the opportunity to understand the loss of control. This can only come from listening to those who have overcome their dependence on alcohol; for example, those who are involved in practising the Alcoholics Anonymous programme.

Social drinkers who do not understand alcoholism will view the out-of-control drinker as someone who has a wish to self-destruct or has no moral backbone. They will make comments like, "Why doesn't he stop drinking like that and just have one or two?" or, "Can't she see what she is doing to herself?" or, "Where is your willpower? Pull yourself together!" Because these well-meaning people have the power to choose how they will drink, they view the alcoholic as someone who has got clear-cut, easy choices. They do not perceive that he has crossed that subtle, fine line between stress-relief drinking and dependence on alcohol. They do not understand the compulsion of someone who has become 'hooked', who is struggling with that overwhelming urge to drink. It is, I believe, very important that we have some appreciation of the intensity of that pull to experience the recurrence of the intoxicating feeling; that is, if we are interested in helping someone who is alcoholic.

In fact, alcoholism is just that: a profound, obsessive urge to repeat the experience of being intoxicated. It is so strong that it usually overpowers the sufferer's strength of will to do anything about it — other than drink or take some other form of medication. (In other areas of their lives, many alcoholics will prove themselves to be extremely strong-willed.) An alcoholic will be so obsessed with the search for that 'high' that it transcends all his other needs. His need to love and be loved, his need to feel worthwhile, for food, for sexual relationships, even his need to survive; all these needs become secondary to the need to repeat that powerful, overwhelming feeling.

In the early stages of the illness, the budding alcoholic and others can be conned into believing that there is not really a drinking problem. There may be periods of remission: he may carefully abstain or control his drinking for periods of time — days, weeks, even months in some cases. If he is alcoholic, it is inevitable that there will be another period of uncontrolled drinking — unless he has recognised his need for help. For others there is no remission at all. Once they have experienced that loss of control, it keeps on happening over and over again. Some alcoholics report being out of control from the first drink. A number state that the disease was obviously lying latent for some time before they first sensed their powerlessness over alcohol.

Many social drinkers think that it is stress that causes an alcoholic to drink. He may have entered into alcoholism by the route of stress-relief drinking. Indeed he may accuse others of causing his drinking by creating upset. Richard Heilman states in his paper, *Early Recognition of Alcoholism and Other Drug Dependence* — "The urge to become intoxicated becomes independent of any other aspects of our lives. Tension, depression, excitement, etc. can stimulate the urge or need to 'take' something, but are not necessary." The compelling need to drink can trigger itself off. Any reason given is often a justification created by the drinker to make himself feel more comfortable with giving into that urge. It is part of the denial system discussed in the next chapter.

Please note, alcoholics are often unhappy and depressed because of the sense of confusion, isolation and fear of what is happening to them. However, what most people do not realise is that alcohol taken in large quantities acts as a depressant. It is the consumption of alcohol that exacerbates most of the depression — not simply the black feelings that cause the alcoholism.

Alcoholism is Loss of Control

An alcoholic is a person who no longer can choose how he drinks. If he does elect to drink (or take other addictive chemicals) he cannot predict what will be the outcome. Not only has he lost control of his drinking, but when he does drink he loses control of his behaviour. Often, he will not remember incidents because he is on a blackout (a period of alcohol-induced amnesia). At a party, he may uncharacteristically proposition his best friend's wife in front of everyone, argue a point too strongly, publicly insult his wife with a comment that is a little too vivid. Sometimes he is charming, but he can rapidly swing into unpredictable personality changes. Throughout the course of his illness he may well become uncharacteristically dishonest, devious, irresponsible, manipulative, self-centred and insensitive to others.

Someone suffering from alcoholism will continue to drink or take other sedatives despite the fact that his health may be seriously affected; his friendships at risk; his family in disarray; his finances in chaos; his work prospects grim; and the likelihood of legal convictions hang over him.

Alcoholism Destroys the Individual's Ability to Function as a Human Being

It may be that most people will think that the heading above is a very obvious comment. After all, if someone is falling over drunk, wetting himself, slurring his speech, has difficulty in focusing his sight, or cannot walk in a straight line, it is plainly evident that he is unable to function responsibly as a human being.

However, the disintegration of the individual can be more subtle and deeper than this. Often it is not noticed or understood by people who have not experienced alcoholism. Most alcoholics are not continually falling over. Their ability to function can be affected in other ways. They can be 'topped-up' (maintaining a certain amount of alcohol in the system while appearing to behave normally). They can be hung over or 'white-knuckling it' until the next drink. Alcoholics seldom have a good night's sleep. Insomnia and nightmares are often their bedfellows even if they do spend hours in bed avoiding the reality of being awake. As well as being exhausted, they rarely eat properly. All of these conditions affect the concentration.

Most alcoholics find an incredible strength of will to hide the effect of the drinking. For example, managing to turn up for work on time, every day, despite feeling like death warmed up. (It is usually the social drinkers, or those in the later stages of the illness who more often give in to the effects of a hangover and report absent from their place of employment.) Still, despite huge efforts, alcoholics are unable to pay attention, or to work as effectively as they did in the early stages of the illness. They are frightened by their more frequent loss of memory.

Generally, most sufferers of alcoholism are full of shame, guilt, despair, anxiety and remorse. They know that something is wrong. They are disappointed because they have let themselves and others down. They are aware of their deteriorating performance at work, their worsening human relationships. They see themselves as misunderstood by the rest of the population; they feel apart and isolated. They believe they have fallen from grace. Also, at one time alcohol may have lowered inhibitions and enhanced sexual relationships. By the chronic stage of the illness both men and women find themselves unattractive, disinterested and unable to perform sexually.

You may be asking, "Why, if they are feeling so bad, do they not just stop drinking?" Unfortunately, part of the nature of alcoholism is its tendency to deceive and delude its victims. Alcoholics know that they are feeling bad. They do not recognise that it is their dependence on alcohol that is making them feel that way. They can no longer look at themselves and their behaviour objectively. Alcohol has diminished their ability to see clearly what is happening. It is like trying to find one's way while struggling through a thick fog. Often alcoholics honestly believe that drinking is not the problem; that they can stop at any time. They do not understand that alcohol has completely taken over their lives and *that* is what is destroying them. *One of the major characteristics of the illness is the alcoholic's delusion or denial.*

Alcoholism is an Emotional and Spiritual Disorder

Perhaps many professional people would have put this at the top of the list of characteristics of alcoholism. By placing it here I do not intend to diminish its importance but, so often, caring people will 'zoom in' on the underlying emotional issues. They do this without recognising or accepting the primary problems of the physical dependence on alcohol — the denial of the alcoholic concerning his addiction, the distortion of reality or the strength of the compulsion to drink. Unless these are confronted and dealt with first, I do not believe it is possible to face or change the personality disorders. It can take months of abstinence before the recovering alcoholic can emerge from the fog and start to discover who he is and how he feels.

Nevertheless, an integral part of alcoholism is the destruction of the spirit of the individual. After total abstinence, the most important factor in recovery is finding peace with who you are. It is impossible to find that serenity while struggling to control the compulsion to drink. On the other hand, it is difficult to achieve contented sobriety if you are not at ease with yourself.

Every alcoholic is out of touch with his feelings. Alcohol has anaesthetized his pain, his joy, his love, his grief, his anger, his compassion, his fear. He doesn't know who he is. He is estranged from his own self. He uses alcohol to try and feel normal.

I shy away from using the term 'addictive personality'. It seems to suggest that the hundreds of alcoholics, with whom I have worked over the years, are similar in personality. Nothing could be further from the truth. I have worked with introverts and extraverts, the sensitive and not-so-sensitive, intellectuals and physically creative people. However, what our clients do have in common is a high standard of perfectionism, a feeling of not being good enough, and a profound shame of being who they are. That shame has been exacerbated by the addiction but usually it is present long before the alcoholism took off.

In chapter seven, I look at the shame of the alcoholic and his family in much more depth.

Alcoholism is a Dramatic Change of Personality

So often an alcoholic has been described as a 'Jekyll and Hyde' character. Others have been wrongly labelled as schizophrenic. The worst part of living with an alcoholic is never knowing what to expect next; how he is going to behave; or the appropriate way to react to him. The out of control drinker sways from one extreme of behaviour to the other. Gentle, charming people suddenly and unexpectedly become aggressive and insolent. Normally shy, timid individuals swing into overbearing and publicly embarrassing conduct. Very moral people slide into wildly promiscuous behaviour.

Many alcoholics are surprised that a relative or friend can tell so quickly that they have been drinking. Close ones report that they know because of a certain expression in the eyes, a particular way he holds his body, or because there is a different inflection in the voice. It can appear that the drinker has been taken over or possessed. He is not himself when under the influence of alcohol.

In fact, alcoholism produces a split in the personality of the alcoholic, even when he is not drinking: a split between the true self and the addictive self. The more you deny the reality of yourself, the more likely an addiction will take over. Alcoholism is a blotting out of your pain, your life, your reality. It is a long, agonizing struggle between these two parts of the psyche. As long as an addicted drinker struggles against his addictive self, his addiction will win. It is in accepting that negative, destructive, compulsive part of himself that he finds recovery: when he surrenders and asks for help in fighting his addiction.

Alcoholism Brings Loneliness

It is a myth that most alcoholics are down and outs. Probably only 3% fit into this stereotype. In fact, the majority are supported by a family or similar caring network of people. Nevertheless, although there are people around, all alcoholics feel isolated, apart from the rest of the world, and misunderstood. This is partly because of the sufferer's preoccupation with the intoxicating liquor. His need for that comes before his relationships with those who want to love him. He has also become very self-centred. Protective of his need for alcohol, he tries to keep the extent of his dependence from others, becoming defensive and mistrustful of those who try to get close. He emotionally evades life and lives in a kind of 'Walter Mitty' dream world. He fantasizes the way things could be, not connecting with the mainstream of life. His best friend is his bottle and even that has turned against him.

Alcoholism Causes Profound and Painful Turmoil in the Family

Perhaps the individuals who suffer most from the traumas of the disease are those with whom the alcoholic has a close relationship. Family members are often ignored by the helping professions, the drinker demanding most of the attention. Frequently, they are blamed by ignorant people for causing the dependence on alcohol. However, they have probably had to endure the pain of reality more than the alcoholic has because he has been anaesthetized by alcohol and other sedatives much of the time.

There are several chapters in this book devoted to looking at the consequences of alcoholism in the family. Also, we can observe how, because of lack of knowledge, the family can naively help the alcoholic further into the disease because they are over-protective.

In order to help an alcoholic recover, many families will find that they have to change their attitudes and stop being his caretakers. They too need help and support in recovering from this ravaging illness. Sadly, they rarely get it. This includes both children and adults.

Alcoholism is an Illness Which Can be Arrested

There is no known cure for alcoholism. When I use the word 'recovery', I mean an arresting of the disease — not a permanent healing. Once someone has the illness *it is in his system for the rest of his life*. However, that does not mean he has to be permanently drunk for the remainder of his days on earth. Alcoholics can find, and continue to live, a fulfilling life as long as they totally abstain from using any alcohol or other sedative drugs. If a recovering alcoholic starts to use prescribed sedatives, it is highly likely that he will soon be back on the booze. The early days of recovery are not easy. The urge to return to drinking can be overwhelming. Taking it one day at a time, with the support of self-help groups like Alcoholics Anonymous, makes the path smoother. Few alcoholics manage to establish and maintain recovery on their own.

You may have noticed that I use the term 'recovering' alcoholic rather than 'recovered'. Recovery is a way of life that has to be worked at constantly. There is always a potential for relapse. An alcoholic can never afford to be complacent or believe that he has his addiction beaten. If he drinks again, the loss of control could so easily result in his death. Hence my use of the adjective 'recovering'. It gives no illusion of false hope. It illustrates that *recovery from this illness is a process which goes on throughout life; it is not an instant occurrence.* Alcohol is a dangerous substance for the alcoholic. It is as life-threatening as heroin is to the addict. Yet, many people (alcoholic and non-alcoholic) who can see the sense in a drug-dependent person giving up narcotics, still try to encourage the out-of-control drinker to drink moderately. I can only view this as highly irresponsible behaviour. I have seen too many people die from this disease.

Alcoholism Could be Recognised Much Sooner Than it is

So much anguish and pain, destruction, waste, and needless expense could be prevented if only a number of influential people would stop hiding from the reality of alcoholism in our society. If only they would open their eyes to see that it is possible to greatly reduce the resulting devastation. The illness could be arrested before it destroys so much. What needs to happen is that we open our minds and improve our awareness. We do that by asking questions of people who understand the disease, by talking openly, by passing on our knowledge, by breaking the national conspiracy of silence. There is a lot of information available for those who are interested.

For example, it is known by some that it is possible to recognise dependence on alcohol much earlier than it normally is. There are eight symptoms of the type of drinking of someone who is psychologically dependent on alcohol. This pattern is characteristic of all alcoholics from all backgrounds and all ages. These signs all occur in the early stages of the illness.

Pre-occupation

A person who has become dependent on alcohol often has drinki~ uppermost in his mind. He will think or talk about it when he sh~ be concerned with other matters. He will find all sorts of excv~

have the next drink. That experience of 'getting high' or being intoxicated, becomes a priority in his life. He wants to keep repeating that sensation. This is the first stage of dependence on the drug. Pre-occupation is a characteristic that repeats itself over and over again throughout the progression of the illness.

Increased Tolerance

Contrary to most people's assumption, the budding alcoholic is often the person at the end of the party who is relatively sober, looking after everyone else, seeing them home. In the early stages, he has probably a reputation for being able to 'hold his drink' or to 'drink everyone else under the table'. At this time he is often popular and admired for the way he behaves. Although he drinks more than the social drinker, he can remain remarkably efficient. It is in the final stages of the illness that his tolerance decreases and his behaviour appears more and more out of control. However, in the beginning, the more he searches for that 'high', the more he has to drink to find it, the more his tolerance develops. It is almost as though the disease is playing a tantalising game with him.

Gulping Drinks

Because he wants to get that elusive feeling as quickly as possible, the alcoholic will knock back his booze to get the effect more rapidly. The person dependent on alcohol will often order his drinks in large quantities: double whiskies, double vodkas, double gins. Although there are alcoholics who prefer beer, they are few because of the volume that needs to be consumed before the desired effect is achieved. The time spent in the loo is resented because it wastes what is considered by the drinker as 'good drinking time'! An alcoholic will experiment with alcohol in order to find the way that he can achieve the optimum in pleasurable response.

He is often impatient with those who drink slowly. Perhaps he will take on the responsibility of ordering the next round, knocking back a large one while he is waiting for the barmaid to complete the order. Another alternative is to make an excuse to disappear to the t, nip to the bar next door and have a couple of quick ones while hers are casually sipping their original drinks. The alcoholic cook or housewife will keep making excuses to slip out to the kitchen to have a sneaky drink while the guests are pre-occupied with conversation or food.

Drinking Alone

Most people drink because it is sociable to do so. Occasionally, they might have a drink on their own. Every alcoholic will find a reason to drink on his own, even when other people are around and not drinking. He may choose to go out to his garage or to his bedroom to do so. The effect that alcohol gives him has become much more important than his relationship with other people. He may pop into the pub under the guise of meeting friends. However, he becomes less and less interested in the others as his impatience urges him to reach for that 'high'.

Use as a Medicine

Once an alcoholic has experienced the extreme pleasure that alcohol gives him, he often thinks of this beverage as the answer to all problems — something which will heal all ills. He will use it to help relieve tension or anxiety, he will use it to ease the physical symptoms of any illness he has. He comes to view it as a panacea. He depends on it to make him feel better in any stressful situation. He believes that it has become his best friend.

Periods of Amnesia

These are known as blackouts. By this I do not mean passing out (as in fainting), but the recognition of being unable to recall certain periods of time. This is caused by consuming large amounts of alcohol. As the illness progresses, these blackouts become more frequent. Such occurrences may include an alcoholic waking up in a strange bed and not remembering how he got there; or making a telephone call to a friend only to find that he had made the call already two or three hours ago; or one man I knew admitted himself for treatment because he had no recollection of a trans-Atlantic flight — and he was the pilot!

Protecting the Supply

As with any other drug dependence, an alcoholic often likes

more secure in the knowledge that alcohol is available should he want it. He believes he may need it to calm him down if he gets agitated, or, alternatively, he may need it to help him get going, to 'pep' him up. He will probably make sure that there is easy access to alcohol at home, at work and even in the car. He will become quite ingenious at trying to disguise this from other people. The alcoholic housewife learns how to buy her sherry from the housekeeping money and conceal it from the family by storing it in a vinegar bottle at the back of the food cupboard. Other alcoholics will hide their supply in cavities between the floorboards, in holes dug in the garden, in the work shed disguised as paintstripper or tucked in the water cistern — to name but a few!

Overwhelmed by the Urge to Drink

An alcoholic will often end up drinking more than he planned. His drinking is usually different from what he would like it to be. He wants the effect, but he doesn't want the loss of control which goes with it. As an example, a woman alcoholic may buy in some bottles of her husband's favourite wine to celebrate a special occasion with friends. She decides to reward herself with a couple of glasses at lunchtime and finds that she has to replenish the stock because she drinks the whole amount. She had not planned this. The urge to drink superceded thought. The male alcoholic may stop off at a pub on the way home from work fully intending to have a couple of drinks. Three hours later he weaves his way back to an exasperated wife who has thrown out yet another ruined meal. He drank far more than he intended to. The urge to drink more and seek intoxication had overcome him.

Experts believe that if a person shows four or more of the above symptoms repeated over a period of time, then there is absolutely no question that he is alcoholic. The consistent need to 'get high' shows that he is psychologically dependent on alcohol. Once he has a drinking pattern with these symptoms, it is unlikely that he will be able to return to social drinking. The only way out is total abstinence ᵐm all chemicals which change the mood. The alternative is ⁻ioration of health, of psychological wellbeing, of family ⁿships, friendships, of efficiency at work, and finances.

Probably an early insanity or an early death will follow this pattern. *However, the alcoholic is unlikely to reach this conclusion on his own. As I have mentioned before, he is caught up in a web of denial and delusion. He needs other people to help make him aware that he has the illness and that he has the option to recover.*

Take the derelict in the gutter, lying close to insanity or death; rejected by his family, friends and society. He once exhibited those early symptoms. He hasn't recently, suddenly become an alcoholic. Nor did it happen five years ago when he became unemployed, nor ten years ago when his wife divorced him, nor fifteen years ago when he was 'promoted sideways' instead of getting a senior management position. It was twenty to twenty-five years ago that he was showing these symptoms. (In men it can take this time for the disease to develop; with women it can be less than ten years.) He was having blackouts and sneaking his drinks all that time ago. However, no one is likely to have mentioned his problem with alcohol until the later stages of the disease. By this time, his denial system has become so intact that it may have been impossible to reach him. Perhaps if some knowledgeable person had intervened twenty years ago, he may now be sober, healthy, holding down a responsible job and enjoying his family — today.

Alcoholism is a Treatable Illness

A number of alcoholics are dismissed by many as being helpless cases, as having a death wish. Sadly, it is largely because of this ignorance that the majority of alcoholics do, in fact, die from their disease. Many death certificates use euphemisms when the primary agent for the fatality was alcoholism. If only it had been recognised. If only the individual had had an opportunity to receive treatment. He *may* have been alive today.

With the aid of self-help organisations like Alcoholics Anonymous and treatment centres which advocate total abstinence, many alcoholics do arrest the illness. Not only do they stop drinking but they find a more peaceful, fulfilling and constructive way of life

2

Why do People Deny Being Alcoholic?

He does not think there is anything the matter with him
because
    one of the things that is
    the matter with him
    is that he does not think that there is anything
    the matter with him
therefore
    we have to help him realize that
    the fact that he does not think there is anything
    the matter with him
    is one of the things that is
    the matter with him

Knots, R. D. Laing

One of the alcoholics who had the most profound impact on me in my
early days as a counsellor was George. George, when he was admitted
to treatment, was suffering from cirrhosis of the liver. He had been
told that if he continued to drink alcohol he would be dead within a
very short period of time. That ill-looking man stayed in treatment for
four days. He discharged himself, saying he wanted to go home, that
he wouldn't drink, that he had never really had a problem with alcohol
anyway. In the last few weeks he had perhaps been drinking a bit too
much, but it was the anniversary of his son's death. Anybody would
want to drown their sorrows in his position. However, he had learned
lesson; he didn't need treatment; he didn't intend to drink ever

again. (I believe he sincerely meant that at the time.) Six weeks later I had a telephone call from his wife, Sarah. George was dead (aged 48). He had drunk alcohol every day since leaving treatment.

Some time after the funeral Sarah came to visit me. She needed to talk. Sarah and George had been married for twenty-two years. Right from the beginning she had been aware that alcohol had played a very important part in his life. Twice in the early years she had tried to talk to him about it but he had just laughed at her, pointing out several of their friends who obviously drank much more than he did. She agreed that she was probably making too big an issue of it and put it to the back of her mind. Nevertheless, she kept a quiet eye on him and for some time there was no great problem.

George was a banker. He did extremely well in his work when he was in his early thirties and received several promotions. However, Sarah was becoming more anxious because his drinking was increasing. She began to find the odd empty bottle hidden in the attic or the garden shed. She decided there was no point talking to him about it because he became so angry and defensive and accused her of nagging. After a dinner party with friends, when he publicly ridiculed an actress friend of theirs about her latest performance, Sarah tried to talk to his best friend. He was kind and supportive, but there was no way that he was going to agree that his friend George had a drinking problem. After all, he had the reputation of being one of the town's up-and-coming successful young bankers. Didn't Sarah realise what stress he was under? He had been working so hard. Perhaps she should arrange a holiday for them both. She did so and he spent most of the vacation in the bar.

Since his early forties George had obviously gone into a slow but steady decline. He stopped getting any promotion at work; people who had worked under him were now his bosses. Their only son died (aged fourteen) in a car accident while on holiday with some friends. George disappeared for three weeks after the funeral, leaving Sarah to grieve on her own. He emerged from a drinking binge to find someone else in his job. Sarah discovered later that he had been given several warnings because of absences and irresponsible decisions which had cost his employers a lot of money. Sarah became the breadwinner and the housekeeper, she looked after George who, despite all her effo to stop him, somehow managed to get hold of alcohol and dri

After a few feeble attempts, he gave up looking for work. He rationalised that he was an independent spirit and needed to be his own boss. He had great ideas about setting up his own business. However, it never materialised.

George died really believing that life had conspired to give him a raw deal. His denial was so profound that he genuinely was unable to see his problem — that he was out of control with alcohol and had been for some time. He believed that drinking was the only thing that helped him to cope. He died as a result of his alcoholism, apparently still convinced of that belief.

Three Factors Which Help Cause the Denial

When I was working out the plan for this book, I decided that it was important to look closely at the whole issue of the denial of a person who suffers from alcoholism. It is a factor which is notoriously well known to anyone who has a fleeting acquaintance with the problem. Yet, it is often ignored or dismissed as having little importance by many professionals and friends who try to help the alcoholic. Naively, they believe him when he innocently declares that he never has more than a couple of drinks each day. Even when he is stinking of the stuff! All too easily, we can forget how deluded he is. Often, we do not understand that the addiction has cunningly distorted his thinking.

Others perceive the denial as lying, an obvious side-stepping and escape from taking any responsibility for harmful actions. For example, violent arguments may be described as a minor disagreement, or caused by the wife's bad temper, or simply ignored altogether. 'Slightly tipsy' may be the term used by a mother when she mentions her visit to her son's school and embarrasses him by staggering, smelling of alcohol, slurring her speech and loudly and publicly asking his best friend if he is still a virgin.

Obviously, it is understandable that people react towards this kind of behaviour with hostility. We dislike lying or irresponsible and embarrassing behaviour; particularly in people we are close to. It ames us. Families are often dismayed by the drinker's distortion of ity. They frequently start to question their own sanity because he onvinced his perception is right.

The alcoholic is often perplexed because he finds himself rejected. The morning after the night before can bring cold shoulders from his relatives, but he doesn't remember the embarrassing scenes, the broken coffee table, the violent arguments. His awareness of reality has been impaired by the alcohol in his system. He genuinely does not know how serious his problem has become. He denies his alcoholism for these three reasons.

The Stigma of Alcoholism

The disease alcoholism still carries a deep sense of disgrace with it. Most people today drink alcoholic beverages. In our society, most adults are expected to drink alcohol. Some have to suffer a great deal of criticism if they do not. The drinks industry 'pushes' alcohol with a lot of pressure through media advertising campaigns.

Yet, although we strongly encourage people to drink, we disapprove, object to or ostracise those who behave in a 'different', perhaps embarrassing way, under the influence of alcohol. We sneer at those who 'cannot handle it'.

One reason why alcoholics deny their problems is because of the fear of being stigmatised by their fellow human beings.

The No-Talking Rule

I don't believe that an alcoholic will recover from this illness unless he is helped to become aware of the extent of his denial. As long as he is only listening to the delusions of his illness and believes that his drinking is not that bad really, he will continue to imbibe.

Sadly, his circle of friends and colleagues will continue to feed that delusion because they don't talk to him about inappropriate behaviour when he has been drinking. They may be gossiping amongst themselves about how embarrassing it was when he knocked over the Christmas tree, broke the lights and destroyed a number of presents, thus causing his wife to burst into tears, not to mention spoiling the atmosphere of the party. With him they made light of it. The budding alcoholic was probably in a blackout when it happened. He had no recollection of the incident and he accused his wife exaggerating when she tackled him the next morning. So, she t line of least resistance and learns to tiptoe around him as t on eggshells. She does this because she believes his taunts that it is her fault that he is drinking, and because she gets no support from their friends.

Even in a work situation, people will not address the drinking problem directly. If it starts to cause problems in the job, two things may happen. The worker will be sacked, or colleagues will close ranks and cover up for the alcoholic, concealing his irresponsible behaviour. The latter is more likely to happen with those who have a high status job.

At the time when the alcoholic starts to face reality, friends, family, even those in the helping professions, can react defensively. "You, alcoholic? Don't be ridiculous!" Such soothing, wonderful words to a person who is craving a drink!

The second reason that an alcoholic denies his problem is because those close to him do little to help. In fact, through misplaced loyalty, they enable him further into the disease by allowing him to continue to be deluded. Because they don't understand the nature of the disease, they neglect to describe what is actually happening.

As you will see from chapter five, the most helpful way to help an alcoholic is to tell him about his drinking — when he is sober.

The Seductiveness of the Addiction

Alcohol, taken in large amounts, impairs the individual's awareness. It numbs his feelings, blunts his perceptions, blanks out his memory and destroys his sensitivity to others. He is living in a fog. He cannot see what is going on around him. At times he genuinely cannot remember what has happened because of blackouts (periods of alcohol-induced amnesia).

Occasionally he may have a vague awareness that alcohol is causing some problems in his life, but he is in a conflict. He loves to drink because for a while it makes him feel wonderful. He has a choice — reject drinking or reject the reality which is warning him of damaged relationships or impaired work efficiency. Some *do* choose to give up drinking, especially if there are people in their lives who keep confronting the alcoholic with the real state of his life. Others ⁻ct to listen to the addiction and to reject that reality. The further the illness he goes, the more he wants to hide from the pain of the

As long as he is able to justify his drinking and say it is not really that bad; as long as he believes he can control alcohol; as long as he blots out the truth he is going to progress further and further into the illness. Thus, drawing nearer to insanity, dereliction and death.

A third reason that an alcoholic continues to deny his alcoholism is his obsession with the continuation of achieving that 'high'. His addiction keeps telling him it is more important to him than reality.

Forms of Denial

When a person experiences a painful situation in life, it is a natural human response to deny its existence, initially. This happens with a great loss such as the death of a loved one, the break-up of a relationship or a serious illness. Addictions of all sorts are also denied — not just alcoholism. Heroin addicts hide their dependence on the drug; gamblers avoid talking about the 'high' that winning gives them; overeaters refuse to admit to the amount of food they are eating; heavy smokers do not own their dependence on nicotine. Every addict develops a denial system to justify the continuing use of the substance he is dependent upon. An alcoholic can deny his alcoholism in several ways:

He may deny or minimise the amount of alcohol he is drinking or the number of pills he takes

He may do this by hiding bottles, sneaking drinks, lying, or deceiving himself into believing he is drinking much less. He may talk of having a couple of drinks and believe it. The reality in this case is probably two tumblers-full of spirits! A slight distortion of the truth!

He will deny the extent of his dependence on alcohol and chemicals and the obsession with finding that exciting feeling

He will find all sorts of excuses or reasons to drink. It could be because it's cold, it's hot, he's unhappy, he is happy, he's drowning his sorro he's celebrating. These are produced to justify his drinking to hir as much as anyone else.

He avoids the subject

Alcoholics become extremely adroit at avoiding talking about their drinking. They seem to develop special antennae which sense when the subject is about to come up. They react to it by getting out of the room, changing the subject quickly or looking so hurt that you have dared to raise the subject. Sometimes, the alcoholic will take the attitude of, "Well, if you don't trust me, I may as well go and get drunk, anyway!" So often, concerned persons can end up feeling guilty for mentioning the word 'drink'.

He may blame others

He manages to take the focus off himself by twisting things around and blaming others for causing so much stress in his life. He excuses his drinking by pointing the finger at others. He actually sees himself as a victim and believes that circumstances have conspired against him. He justifies his need to drink in order to relieve the tension. He believes that alcohol is the only thing that will make him feel better.

Others fall into the trap and encourage this denial by believing that the drinking is someone's or something's fault. A death or a tragic accident will be blamed; stress at work will be produced as a reason; a nagging wife, an unsympathetic father, rebellious children, are all common reasons given why the alcoholic drinks.

Please note: Alcoholism is the fault of no one. An alcoholic drinks the way he does because he is in love with the intoxicating feeling it produces. He may well have had some traumatic events in his life; they possibly have provided him with excuses for drinking. He may even be angry at you or have been upset by you. However, no one has the power to make his drinking go out of control. It goes out of control because of that compulsive drive within him.

He denies his feelings and the effects of his drinking on others

A number of relatives have commented bitterly, "If he loved me, he would stop drinking. He wouldn't keep doing this to me." It is highly probable that the alcoholic does love those close to him — he also loves, and tells himself he needs, that alcoholic feeling. He is not fully aware of the effect of his drinking on loved ones. Partners have a habit of talking about it when the alcoholic has been drinking and therefore not hearing too clearly. Quite often, he really doesn't understand why he is receiving hurtful and angry looks from the rest of the family after what was to them a memorable night. He probably doesn't remember that he was obnoxious, embarrassing or out of control.

Most alcoholics do feel extremely guilty about remembered incidents which have happened under the influence of alcohol or other drugs. However, the way that the alcoholic has learned to deal with painful feelings is to anaesthetize them. The more aware of pain caused to others, the more uncomfortable he is; the more he wants to make himself feel better, the more he justifies the need to drink; the more he drinks, the more guilty he feels... It is a vicious circle of repression and denial.

He uses some common myths to convince himself and others that he is not alcoholic

The following section is devoted to describing some of these old wives' tales.

Alcoholics and others who don't want to face the reality of the illness or who don't understand alcoholism, will supply a lot of reasons why someone cannot be suffering from the disease. These are some of the more common justifications and myths.

'ALCOHOLICS ARE DOWN AND OUTS'

As mentioned before, the common picture of an alcoholic is of a lonely old man, lying on the park bench muttering to himself, his clothes tied together with string, smelling of stale booze and clutching his bottle of cheap red wine. The great majority of alcoholics do not fit into this stereotype at all. Most of them are involved in family life, holding down a good job, although they are having problems because of their drinking.

The forsaken person in the gutter is often in the final stages of the illness. It has taken him years to get to that point. Others have died as a result of their drinking long before that happens.

'I'M A WOMAN!'

Women alcoholics suffer an even greater stigmatisation than do their male counterparts. Society screws up its nose in disgust at the woman who is out of control! Drunkenness is accepted in some quarters as quite 'macho'. However, it is definitely seen as a very unfeminine activity in all sections of our culture. Nevertheless, the number of alcoholic women from all walks of life is increasing.

As a result of the more obvious stigmatising of women alcoholics, the female denial system can be even more intact than that of a man. Many cling on to the delusion that their drinking is ladylike!! Forgotten is the swigging from the bottle, the falling over, the swearing loudly, the food-stained smelling clothes and the embarrassment of the family. Also, more women alcoholics tend to be dependent on tranquillizers as well as alcohol. They will find themselves substituting alcohol for the prescribed medicine and vice versa. Thus, they can then con themselves and others that they can't possibly be alcoholic because they actually drink very little. Of course, they are omitting to mention that they are taking large quantities of tranquillizers instead.

'HE ONLY DRINKS AT WEEKENDS'

A number of wives have said this to me, trying to convince themselves and others, that their husbands couldn't possibly be alcoholic. Many people still want to cling on to that common fallacy that in order to be an alcoholic, you have to drink great quantities every day.

Many alcoholics can go for long periods of time without a drink. Some even 'stay dry' for weeks, months, even years. The questions to ask are not when or how often, but what happens when he drinks? How does he behave? Does his personality change? Does he behave in ways which are alien to him? Does he drink more than he intends to? Does he live for the weekend, anticipating the feeling he gets from alcohol? Would his weekend be ruined if he didn't drink? If you've answered 'yes' to any of these questions, it is highly likely that he is alcoholic.

'HE ONLY DRINKS BEER'

Beer is as alcoholic as gin, whisky, vodka or wine is alcoholic. It is the chemical ethyl alcohol that alcoholics are addicted to. One pint of beer has about the same alcohol content as a nip of whisky. Again, it is not **what** someone drinks that is important, it is **why** someone drinks it. Flavour is not all that important to alcoholics. In fact, many of those addicted to alcohol report that they do not like the taste, it is the feeling that they go for.

'I DON'T DRINK IN THE MORNINGS'

Another myth about alcoholics is that they **have** to drink in the mornings. In the later stages of the illness, the drinker may need a 'morning drink' to get going. However, alcoholism can be developing a long time before this happens.

Also, an alcoholic in the later stages of the illness can lose all sense of time structure. He may live by night and 'sleep' by day. Having a drink when everyone else is having lunch can be justified as not being a morning drinker. However, that lunch may well be just at the time the alcoholic is surfacing for the day! He still needs it to get going or to settle the shakes.

'SHE STOPS DRINKING FOR MONTHS AT A TIME'

A lady I know admitted herself for treatment. Her husband was most indignant. He had great difficulty in accepting her alcoholism because she had periods when she was 'on the wagon' for months. Again, his stereotype of an alcoholic was of a male person who drank all the time.

It is reasonably easy for an alcoholic to stop drinking for a period of time. Most people don't have to do this; they suddenly abstain from drinking because it is giving them problems. Many alcoholics will cease drinking to prove to themselves, and others, that they are still in control. However, it is when they do drink that the problems start. For a while it may look under control but if the person is a compulsive drinker, loss of control is inevitable. A period of 'light drinking' will inevitably be followed by a 'heavy bender'.

If someone is alcoholic and is surviving a period of enforced abstinence, family members are often heard to mutter about the nervousness, irritability and depression of the drinker. I often hear comments about, "He's nicer when he's drinking". Social drinkers who haven't had a drink for a period of time don't go through this. Alcohol is not that important to them. It doesn't preoccupy their minds.

'HE'S TOO YOUNG'

Alcoholism does not happen to those in their fifties or sixties only, as many people believe. There are more and more young people joinin~ groups like Alcoholics Anonymous. Loss of control can happen at ~ age. I've worked with several young people of fifteen and sixtee~

are dependent on alcohol. I've heard others report that they vividly remember their first drink at eleven or twelve years of age. The feeling they received from that liquid made such a big impact on them, and they were so pre-occupied with it, that they had to go back and have some more: the beginnings of loss of control. There is a subtle difference between this reaction and that of an adolescent who drinks for bravado and to impress his friends. He may enjoy the feeling, but it does not become an obsession.

'I'VE STILL GOT A JOB'

Work is usually one of the last things to be affected by alcoholism. The family will have been through misery by the time the alcoholic starts to get into trouble with the results of his drinking at work. The compulsive drinker will have exhibited a number of incidents of being out of control with his drinking at home. Don't be conned by comments like, "I can't be alcoholic because I haven't lost my job". The stock answer to that is, "yet!" Unless he gets help in arresting his illness, his work will suffer and he may well lose it.

'MY DOCTOR WOULD HAVE TOLD ME'

Please don't buy into this one. So many people do. It's very common justification for continuing to drink. Doctors are busy people. Also, it is a very rare occurrence when an alcoholic goes along to his doctor's surgery and talks openly and honestly about his drinking. Usually he has no intention of giving up the search for that intensely pleasurable feeling. Probably he will chat to the doctor about all sorts of physical ailments, carefully avoiding talking about his drinking. If the physician does probe into that area, the amount consumed will probably be greatly minimised. The patient may even manipulate the doctor into saying that it is O.K. for him to have a couple of glasses of wine with his meal. A typical alcoholic will interpret that as being complete medical approval of his drinking. "My doctor says it's O.K.". It is important that the doctor hears the family's picture of reality — if he is to help the alcoholic.

'I DON'T DRINK AS MUCH AS TOM, OR DICK, OR HARRIET'

While some alcoholics do develop a high tolerance to alcohol, others ʼt. The amount drunk is not important. It is what happens when nks. Indeed, some social drinkers appear to be able to consume large quantities and not become psychologically dependent on alcohol. They can take it or leave it. Probably, they are also quite open about their drinking. They don't deny. Also, although drinking large quantities of alcohol affects the way they behave, it is unlikely that they will go through a major personality change. If the heavy drinker does get into trouble with his drinking he will take it in hand and cut down. An alcoholic can't do that. He continues to drink, despite the fact that he is having problems.

While reading this chapter, I hope that it has become more obvious that if we are to help more alcoholics recover from this illness, not only do we need some understanding of what alcoholism is, we have to understand the denial — an integral part of this illness. If we really want to help someone who is alcoholic, then we have to help him face and accept that denial system so that he can start to face reality. Unless he does that, he will not get well. His addiction will stay in control.

However, nothing with alcoholism is simple. Often, in order to reach the alcoholic, we first of all have to work through the complicated cobweb of denial created by his family or other caring persons. Most alcoholics have a protective network of people desperately trying to help but, because they too are caught up in the trap of denial and lack knowledge, are enabling him further into the illness; often into the chronic stages and possibly towards death.

Part II
The Family and Alcoholism

3

Peace at What Cost?

"An illness of this sort... involves those about us in a way no other human sickness can. If a person has cancer all are sorry for him and no one is angry or hurt. But not so with the alcoholic illness, for with it, there goes annihilation of all the things worthwhile in life. It engulfs all whose lives touch the sufferer's. It brings misunderstanding, fierce resentment, financial insecurity, disgusted friends and employers, warped lives of blameless children, sad wives and parents — anyone can increase the list."   *Alcoholics Anonymous*

One of the main destructive forces which greatly contributes to the extent of alcoholism in our society is its vast denial system. Previously, I discussed the denial of the alcoholic, but, I want to stress that every alcoholic is surrounded by a structure of individuals and groups who collude in an unrecognised avoidance of reality which enables him into the chronic stages of the illness; quite often towards insanity or death. Usually this is caused by ignorance, the fear of the stigma of alcoholism and a refusal to face the facts.

A Conspiracy of Silence

Generally, we avoid talking about the issue of addiction to alcohol. Perhaps for many of us the problem is too close to home.

The Government, managers of industry, and trade unionists evade the truth which highlights how much the illness is costing the country in terms of lost working hours, accidents, and crazy decisions made under the influence of alcohol. The legal profession fails to recognise how many people they keep sending back to prison; people who are alcoholic, who only behave in an anti-social way when they are drinking; people who, when their real problem is addressed and they are given the right help, will probably learn to behave in a responsible manner. Many journalists will write screeds on the horror and drama of drug addiction, yet shrink away from the equally appalling tales concerning the truth about alcoholism. Often, doctors are unsuccessful at recognising the symptoms of alcoholism because they have had little education about this disease and do not know what questions to ask.

Against this unsupportive background, the family and friends of an alcoholic form a tight-knit and even more protective network. Through the best of intentions, they try to help the alcoholic. Nevertheless, to themselves, as well as to the outside world, they deny the extent of the problem. They present a façade which belies the anguish and torment within. They believe that it would be disloyal to discuss the reality of the situation. Also, they are frightened to do so because the belief is that if they cause any upset it will provoke more drinking. Unfortunately, they, too, become involved in that conspiracy of silence. Parents, siblings, spouses, children, friends, colleagues may all play their part in providing a shielding, but destructive, environment. They too, obey the fatal no-talking rule.

Contrary to what the myth would have us believe, an alcoholic is rarely a loner. Usually he is surrounded by a network of people who are concerned and doing their best to help him. Most of us have been brought up to believe that if we care for a person, we try to look after him, particularly if he is suffering. Someone who is dependent on alcohol needs attentive people in a very special way. If he did not have their protection, he would not be able to continue with his addiction and survive. However, the more a family or group of close friends protect and cover up for an alcoholic, the more they are cushioning him from facing reality. They become his caretakers and unwittingly take all responsibility away from him, thus, enabling him further into the illness. As a result of their propping him up, he is hindered from facing the consequences of his behaviour. He continues to deceive himself about the seriousness of his dependence on alcohol.

Concerned persons can become obsessed by the alcoholic, entering into a game where no one wins; where each person plays out a role, trying in vain to control the alcoholic's drinking. Amazingly, this pattern, with slight deviations, repeats itself across the board of a very large cross-section of families which contain a problem drinker.

The family I discuss here is an example where the man is suffering from the disease. Where the alcoholic is a woman, events take a similar course. However, in my experience, male partners tend to leave alcoholic wives more than spouses of alcoholic men.

The Role of the Alcoholic

An alcoholic is always the centre of attention of the family where he belongs. The nature of his illness makes him loud, unpredictable, worrying, self-centred, demanding, deceitful, embarrassing and intimidating. Close ones respond by being wary, watchful and over-protective. Family functions tend to be geared around his state of drunkenness or sobriety. Holidays may be cancelled if he is drinking too much. Meal times may be changed to fit in with his longer and longer visits to the pub. The children may learn to stay in their rooms because of the aggressive, sometimes even violent, arguments between their parents. They may stop taking friends home and even find sanctuary in someone else's house where the atmosphere is more peaceful and secure.

If, in the early days, relatives tried to discuss his drinking with him, they now no longer do so. They have learned that it is not worth the hassle. The alcoholic either became so angry and drunk on his resentment or made them feel so guilty for daring to suggest his drinking was a problem. They vowed they would never mention it again. The guilt could be provoked just by hurt looks or somehow subtly blaming them for causing so much stress in his life that he had to drink to ease the pain! In fact, his alcoholically insane thinking will cause him to manipulate his family so that he can justify his drinking. Sometimes, he may deliberately incite an argument with his wife so that she can take the blame for his rushing out, slamming the door and heading for the pub or the nearest bottle. His friends (often people who drink like he does) will then be entertained with long, plausible stories about how irrational and impossible his partner's behaviour is.

He receives a great deal of sympathy and everyone agrees that if they had a marriage like his, they would be driven to drink too!

As a result, the family have learned to tiptoe around him as though on egg-shells. They are frightened of doing anything that will rock the boat. They do not understand the disease concept, so they believe his accusations that somehow the drinking is their fault. They are unaware that the reason he drinks the stuff in that way is because he is powerless to do anything else. Alcohol is in control of him.

I mentioned in the last chapter that one of the main characteristics of the disease alcoholism is denial. At this later stage of the illness, the alcoholic is greatly deluded. Rarely does he see that he has a problem or admit that his drinking is out of control. Sometimes he genuinely cannot remember how he behaved the night before because of a black-out (temporary alcohol-induced amnesia). Usually, he sees himself as a victim of other people's behaviour. He will avoid talking about his drinking but, if the subject does come up, he will point his finger and blame. To his parents and children, he may moan about his nagging wife; to her he will complain about his over-anxious parents who favour his sister and never understood him as a child. He may even blame his children, accusing them of being ungrateful, uncaring, or 'pains in the neck'.

At work he is becoming more and more irresponsible. His time-keeping is poor; his decision-making less reliable. His colleagues who have respected his hard work and devotion to the firm for the past fifteen years, start to take on more responsibility for him and cover up for his increasing absences. His secretary knows perfectly well what is wrong with him when his wife phones to say that the water cistern has burst and he will be absent from work that day. However, this lady has also been manipulated into believing that he drinks because his marriage partner does not understand him.

Out loud, no one admits what the real problem is. At the same time, everyone is feeling responsible and is trying to protect him from any upset. His children, his parents, his wife, his secretary have all found bottles hidden under the seat of the car, in the filing cabinet, in the fishpond, amongst the paint-stripper in the garage. Everyone is aware of what the problem is — but — nobody discusses it, least of all with the alcoholic; probably not even with each other. Without being openly acknowledged, the no-talking rule has silently been enforced.

Role of the Alcoholic's Partner

Many people who ask for help for their alcoholic, view him as the only problem in the family. They assume that when he stops drinking, everything will be 'normal'. They are unaware that alcoholism is an illness that affects others as well as the person exhibiting the primary symptoms described in chapter one. Alcoholism is a dis-ease of the family. There is a ripple effect which involves more people than the addicted drinker in a great deal of stress.

To the outside world, the wife of an alcoholic may present a very composed, 'put-together' image. Inside, she is suffering the agony of shame, guilt, despair, indecision and feelings of impotence. She has become obsessed, even addicted to her alcoholic. She is no longer an individual in her own right, but an extension of the drinker. She believes the drinking is her fault. This is because she does not understand the disease concept or even acknowledge that he is alcoholic. (She does not know what that means. She thinks it is something that happens in other peoples' families.) Secretly, she agrees with him that she has been a failure as a wife. Hasn't she tried everything she could to stop his drinking? She has been gentle with him, coaxed him, pleaded with him, bullied him, even been violent with him; she has played the game of, "you drink, no sex"; she has hidden his bottles; she has asked the children to keep an eye on him; she has taken control of the purse strings and given him controlled amounts of pocket money. The more she tries, the more he drinks and becomes devious; the more inadequate she feels.

She knows she is a different woman from the one he married. She rarely laughs now, she has become a nag and she has little patience with the children. Also, she finds it very difficult to make decisions. Perhaps he is right? Perhaps she should give up her job; improve her cooking, dress like her friend? Her mother-in-law tells her it must be her fault. He didn't drink like this before he met her. What is it that she is doing wrong? His parents won't even talk to her now.

Thank goodness she has her job because it helps keep her mind off the family problems. She can also make sure that they will have enough money at the end of the week to feed the children. How she hates that journey back home. She gears herself up to cope with whatever happens next. Will he stay out tonight? Will he drink? Did the young ones hear last night's argument? Where is he concealing his bottles now? He cried last week when she told him she was leaving him. She had never seen him cry before, so she promised to stay if he didn't drink; he is so dishonest! She knows he is boozing again. She can smell it. His body reeks of it. She can see it in his eyes, but all his usual hiding places are empty. The last time she found his secret storage space, she poured the contents of the bottles down the sink and was given a black eye for doing just that. Then he expected her to make love to him! She hoped her colleagues believed her when she told them she had slipped and hit her face on the bath tap.

What is happening to her? She no longer appears to have any friends. The last time she and her husband went to a party, she curled up with embarrassment. He became loud, romped around the room, tripped and fell, knocking down the Christmas tree. She has avoided those friends ever since. Also, she has politely declined any recent social invitations. She cannot risk another embarrassing scene like that. Anyway, she has to stay at home to keep an eye on him and there is no way that she can go out on her own, leaving him to look after the children. He is too irresponsible.

This lady is so ashamed. She talks to no one about the reality of the situation. If she talks to her husband, it is usually a bitter attack often ending in a destructive argument. Instead of calmly facing the fact that he has a problem and seeking help, she desperately wastes precious time in trying to find out why he drinks so much. His boss is kept away from discovering what is happening — ("He cannot work today. He has come down with 'flu."). To her parents she will excuse long absences — ("He has been so busy at work recently. All he wants to do with his very precious free time is to relax at home."). Also, to the children who are often perfectly aware of what is going on, she will deny the truth — ("Daddy is tired today. Leave him alone. He needs some peace and quiet."). At times, she even convinces herself that things are not that bad really. Denial is part of the family's behaviour as well as the alcoholic's.

This is typical of the attitudes and actions of many partners of alcoholics. For some reason, they believe that they should have the impossible power of controlling an alcoholic's drinking. They care, so they protect and become caretakers. They are blind to the fact that their shielding roles help sufferers of alcoholism further into the morass of that illness. At the same time, spouses have become isolated themselves, even within their own family. Often, they feel inadequate, guilty, angry and full of fear. Not too many people want to hear this, but I find over and over again that relatives of alcoholics tend to get more emotionally hurt by the alcoholism than the drinker does. After all, he has been anaesthetized for years and isn't completely aware of reality. Wives and husbands have had to live with the continual pain and trauma.

It is the lack of knowledge and information that causes most of the destruction. People react in the way that they think best at the time. Unfortunately, for the sake of finding some peace, partners of alcoholics obey the no-talking rule over and over again. Unless they get help for themselves, they will continue to play out the main role in that seemingly endless conspiracy of silence. Not only have they been involved in a great deal of pain and chaos, but most likely the children have been affected by both parents' behaviour as well.

The Roles That The Children of an Alcoholic Can Play

I entered the field of alcoholism through my previous job as a youth worker. Some of the young people (aged eight upwards) with whom I worked had at least one parent who was in trouble with drinking. Once these youngsters had been given permission to talk, I found them most aware of what was happening in their family. Therefore, when I became an alcoholism counsellor, I was somewhat surprised to be confronted by several indignant parents (alcoholic and non-alcoholic) who insisted that their children did not know about the drinking problem. Through my work with such families, I have been involved with a number of children over the years. Please believe me — they know. They may not put the label of alcoholism on the problem, but they know that their family is different from those of their friends. Children, in my experience, are usually much more aware, honest and upfront about what is going on; much more so than their parents.

However, they have learned from the attitudes and behaviours of their mother and father that there are some unwritten rules that they are expected to obey. One of those rules is that you don't talk about what is going on; sometimes, not even to each other and often not to their friends. Unfortunately, they have also learned that not only do you not talk about the drinking or arguments which ensue, but you don't talk about anything which will rock the boat.

It is quite lonely being the child of an alcoholic. Dad is often too preoccupied with his drinking. Mum is too uptight, obsessed with Dad. Usually the alcoholic is the more popular parent of the two. When he is drinking he is not interested in disciplining the children; when he is sober he eases his feelings of guilt by spoiling them, buying expensive presents, taking them off to exciting places, being fun. Mum, on the other hand, isn't seen as a provider of enjoyment. She is the one who has to be the organiser. Because of her preoccupation with her alcoholic partner, her disciplining is sporadic. Sometimes she takes out on the children her frustrations at the alcoholic. The youngsters can see that Mum has become a nag, and because they have no knowledge of the disease concept, they may believe that she is the cause of Dad's excessive drinking.

Children of alcoholics can also enter into the conspiracy of silence, unwittingly. They, too, can try to maintain the equilibrium by acting out several roles. I will describe some of the typical parts that young people play. Most of them will be involved in a combination of at least two of these, but, usually, each child will be biased towards the characteristics of a major role.

The Rebel

If a parent wishes to talk to me about any of the children then, usually, this is the one that I will hear about. He is the child who will make sure that he gets a lot of attention in the family. He learns that you achieve that in this situation, not by being good, but by creating all sorts of upsets. Probably he will do badly at school. He may be quite bright, but he doesn't make the necessary effort. He may play truant. It would not be unusual if he got into trouble with the police. He may experiment with drugs or alcohol at a very early age.

Within the alcoholic family he can play a very important role. He may be made the scapegoat. His part in helping the alcoholic further into the illness is that he takes the attention off the drinking alcoholic. His rebellions can also provide all sorts of excuses for his parent to drink on. His mother and sister spend a lot of time watching him, trying to control his behaviour, mainly because they do not want the alcoholic upset. Often that parent is prevented from knowing what is really going on. School reports are hidden. The rest of the family is sworn to secrecy about his most recent escapades.

In a strange way, he is the child that I least worry about. Everyone can see he has a problem and if they haven't noticed yet, he will make sure that they will. Eventually, he will probably get some help. Hopefully, that will be provided by someone who has an understanding of the effects of alcoholism on the family, and the great emotional pain that this young person suffers.

I have an even greater concern about the children who fall into the other two categories. On the surface, they look so good. They have learned from their non-alcoholic parent how to present a coping façade to the world. To the uninitiated, these children have no problems. Often, inside, they are actually very mixed up. In part five of this book I will spend more time describing what can happen to children who live within an alcoholic family.

The Responsible Child

This is usually the eldest child or eldest daughter in the family. She responds to the chaos of living in an alcoholic home by being very organised; she assumes a lot of the responsibilities. She will look after the younger children, do a lot of the housework. It is her role to alleviate the stress in the home. She will take on a lot of responsibility for her rebellious brother. At school, she excels, works hard and does everything she can to please her parents. As the peacemaker in the family, she will encourage everyone to lean on her. Sometimes she will sit in the car outside the pub for hours, just to keep Dad happy because that is what he wanted. If he is late back from a night out, she will wait up and prepare a meal for him on his return. I once worked with a seven year old who saw it as her duty to do this every weekend. As the main support to her mother, she will learn to be sensitive to the emotional vibrations and know when to break the news that Daddy is drinking again or that her brother is once more in trouble. She, too, will fall into the trap of lying or covering up for her father because of her misplaced loyalty. She will not talk to him about his drinking because that would disturb the brief period of calm in the family. The name of the game is Peace at any Price. She has learned that well.

The Adjuster

This child does what the label suggests. He just adjusts. He is popular within the family because he is so easy going. This is the young person who sits in a room where his parents are screaming at each other and he doesn't bat an eyelid. From a very early age he has learned to tune-out from scenes like this and escape into his world of fantasy. At the age of eight or nine, the adjusting child will happily travel with his Dad to watch his favourite football team play. After the match, Dad gets thirsty and puts him on the return train by himself, saying he has some business to attend to. The young lad, knowing that he has to change trains at two stations, quietly does what he is told and somehow finds his way home. These kids don't question. He learned in the past that it causes a lot of hassle, so he just accepts. It keeps both parents off his back. There is no way he would talk about the drinking. It is something he is resigned to — just as he is resigned to the geographical moves his parents make in attempts to escape the drinking. Again, he just adjusts without making any queries.

Although I have been highlighting the roles that the children can fall into in this chaotic home, my main concern is for their emotional isolation. Many of the youngsters that I talk to know that it is not constructive to show any type of feeling in their family. They have learned when they have been upset not to expect anyone there to comfort them; when they have become angry they have been punished; when something important has happened at school, their parents may have been too preoccupied to notice. First of all many children of alcoholics learn not to show feelings. Secondly, they learn not to feel. As a result, as they grow into adolescence and early adulthood, this can cause all sorts of problems in the forming of close, intimate relationships.

The Unwritten Rules of an Alcoholic Family

I hope that this chapter has clearly illustrated three points. One, that it is not only the alcoholic that suffers from this illness; all those in close proximity to him do so too. Two, if an alcoholic is to get help, then the family need to break that protective shell. There is a way out of that emotionally paralysed state, but it means recognising and breaking those unacknowledged rules. Three, family members need and deserve as much help as the alcoholic does.

Every family needs to have a set of principles so that it can survive, and so that each individual knows how to function within that group. They may not be written down or even talked about, but each person knows what to expect from the system. For example, everyone knows when meals are scheduled to take place. Also, when there is a family crisis everyone knows who will be the leader or the coper. Other rules may include deciding who is responsible for mowing the lawn, cleaning the car or washing the dishes.

In an alcoholic home all sort of additional rules are added to try and maintain the peace. Many people are shocked when they face up to the reality of them. In their desperate attempts to help, this is how the family has learned to survive with the little knowledge they have. Such a list of unwritten regulations may include:-

— Never talk to the alcoholic about his drinking. It upsets him.

— Never talk to the alcoholic about anything else which might upset him.

— Never talk to anyone outside the home about the drinking. It would be extremely disloyal to the family. If you have to, lie to cover up for him.

— Always consider the alcoholic first in this family. If you are making plans for any family or social activity, check out the state of his drinking. Don't invite friends home if he is likely to be drunk.

— Don't let the alcoholic suffer any discomfort. If he falls flat on his face, vomits down his best suit or knocks the standard lamp over, pick him up, clean him up and tidy up after him.

— The alcoholic is not fit to make any responsible decisions. Don't bother him with any of those. The alcoholic is the child in the family. Everyone else is expected to behave in a responsible manner.

— Anyone else in this family who has a problem is a nuisance. Keep them to yourself. We do not tell each other our personal fears and worries. We have enough to cope with.

—   Mum is in charge of the purse strings and the decision-making.

—   We tolerate aggression and sometimes violence in this family. That is, it is sometimes O.K. for the adults to behave in this manner, but the children are punished if they copy their parents.

—   Although everyone acknowledges it is wrong, we are allowed to play dishonest, manipulative games, especially if it keeps the peace and stops the alcoholic from drinking.

—   We allow the alcoholic to control our moods. When he is happy, we are happy. When he is drinking, aggressive or self-pitying, we are down and withdrawn.

—   The most important issue in this family is to keep the alcoholic from drinking. Everyone and everything else is secondary.

Do any of these rules apply to your family?

Obviously, for the health of both the alcoholic and his family this set of rules has to go. When these are applied, the alcoholic is allowed to continue behaving like an irresponsible child and to progress further into this terminal illness; at the same time, his relatives become more disillusioned and feel more hurt, more fearful, more frustrated and more isolated. Recovery demands that the family set up and practise a completely different set of principles. A suggested guideline is listed in part three of this book.

4

The Caretaker

"It was mostly from the wives and girlfriends of addictive men that I began to understand the nature of loving too much. Their personal histories revealed their need for both the superiority and the suffering they experienced in their 'saviour' role and helped me make sense of the depth of their addiction to a man who was in turn addicted to a substance. It was clear that both partners in these couples were equally in need of help, indeed that both were literally dying of their addictions, he from the effects of chemical abuse, she of the effects of extreme stress."

Women who Love too Much, Robin Norwood

Annie is married to David. No one has acknowledged it yet, but David is an alcoholic. Although he has recently had a drink driving charge and is likely to lose his licence; although at times he has great memory lapses because of his drinking; although his boss has been commenting on his long lunch hours and his increased inefficiency at work; although he is hiding bottles amongst the paint stripper in the garden shed, he doesn't think alcohol is his problem. David believes that Annie is his problem. He is convinced she is the reason he is drinking so much. She appears to have lost interest in life, she has become a nag, she is rejecting him sexually. If she changed, his drinking would go back to normal, he is sure of it.

David really believes that. His drinking buddies believe it too. What's more, Annie is beginning to wonder if his accusations are true.

She is frightened about what is happening to her. She has become violent; she is frightened to go out of the house; she is unable to do her work properly. She cannot clear her head of her obsessions about David and his drinking. She has even found herself praying that he will be killed in a road accident, because that is the only way she can see them getting out of this mess. She loves their two children, but she is so tense, so preoccupied by what he is going to do next, she has almost been unaware of them. She is frightened that she is going crazy. What has happened to her? What has happened to their once happy marriage? Where has she gone wrong? What has she done to cause his terrible drinking? Why does he treat her with such contempt? What has she done to deserve this?

When Annie and David were married twelve years ago, they were very much in love. Annie tended to be very shy and David's fun-loving, outgoing personality brought her out of herself. Before Cathy and Sheila were born, they had a great social life and travelled a lot. Occasionally, David drank heavily at a party and became overbearing and loud, but Annie soon forgot her embarrassment because everybody liked him. He had great charm and a large collection of funny stories. However, when they were on holiday in Majorca, Annie decided enough was enough. David had jumped into the swimming pool, fully dressed, pulling a frightened, sixty-year old lady with him. Having had quite a lot to drink, he was totally insensitive to her fear. Later, he was furious with Annie for commenting about it. He told her she had become a bore and didn't know how to enjoy herself. He walked out, slammed the door and vanished for two days. When he appeared again, he was very drunk and dishevelled and spent what was left of their holiday in bed recovering from a blinding hangover.

Annie still hasn't asked him where he disappeared to during that time. She hasn't enquired about what happened. She hasn't told him how worried and frightened she was on her own with a young baby, not knowing where he was. In fact, she rarely comments about his drinking or his disappearing for days because she is frightened that if she says anything it will upset him and he will disappear on another bender.

Over the years, Annie has become more and more isolated. She hasn't seen her friends for a long time; she has stopped going out socially because she can't bear the embarrassment of watching David become more and more drunk. Anyway, she hasn't got the energy or the desire to dress up or to be sociable. She can't keep that smile fixed on her face any more or pretend that everything is wonderful.

She has her work at the library. She is even losing interest in that. At one time, she was able to forget her family troubles there. Now the obsessive thinking invades her mind even while she is working. She can't escape him anywhere. David visited her there the other day, swaying and smelling of booze, demanding that she call his boss to tell him that he had been taken ill. She made the call, aware all the time that her colleagues were watching.

She has tried to stop him drinking so much. She has attempted to hide his bottles, she has spent hours diluting his whisky with cold tea, she has drunk glass for glass with him in an effort to stop him from drinking the whole bottle. The more she has tried to help him, the more he has drunk, and the more inadequate she feels.

Annie has fallen into the trap that most partners of alcoholics stumble into. She does not know that what David is suffering from is an illness; or that that illness is alcoholism. Unfortunately, she is exhausted and depressed because she has spent so much time trying to solve the problem. She believes that because she loves him she should be able to stop him drinking the way he does. He doesn't, so she sees herself as a wife who has failed, has let her husband down. At one level, she believes she should have the power to fix him.

The Relationship Between Caretaker and Alcoholic

Many of us are brought up to believe that if we care about someone we protect, absorb or stop some of that person's pain, and it may be that we even take responsibility for the well-being of that person. Although I accept that most healthy relationships contain an element of this behaviour, I would suggest that in the extreme it stunts the maturing of both partners. That is often what happens in an alcoholic relationship.

In a partnership where one person is alcoholic, the other usually adopts such a role; that of caretaker. In many cases, that individual has gradually taken on that duty as a way to try and balance the irresponsible behaviour of the alcoholic. Probably, the drinker has encouraged that to happen by blaming others, playing the victim, appearing helpless and unable to cope. Gradually the drinking behaviour gets more and more out of control. Quite often, partners do not even see it as necessary to question the role they play in the relationship. After all, as often stated in this book, alcoholism is an illness and it is normally assumed that sick people need to be taken care of. However, alcoholism contains many paradoxes. One of those paradoxes is that although the alcoholics are sick, perhaps the most destructive event that can happen to them is for someone to mother or nurse them; to assume responsibility for their behaviour; to shield or cover up for them. In short, making their drinking more comfortable for them.

A caretaker gradually makes it her purpose in life to be the protector of the alcoholic. She watches and listens for anything that may upset him. Stepping in, she will make sure that the drinker will not suffer from too much stress in case it sets of a drinking binge. Loved ones learn not to talk about the drinking or subsequent drinking behaviour. When they have done so, the alcoholic has sulked, responded aggressively, blamed them, put them down or reacted by going out and getting plastered — just to show them!

Because she cares and wants to help, the alcoholic's partner will try to control the drinking. She may do this in several of the following ways:

— Pleading;

— Hiding bottles, locking drinks cabinets, marking bottles or pouring alcohol down the sink;

— Taking charge of the finances, giving out pocket money when he is a good boy, or covering any debts;

— Being provocative, yielding, sexy or playing the game of, "You drink, no sex";

— Drinking drink for drink with him either with the attitude of, "If you can't beat him, join him", or with the belief that she is helping by consuming half the bottle, thus reducing the alcoholic's intake;

— Lying to the boss, the children, his parents, their friends;

— Cleaning up after him or taking on his responsibilities in the home;

— Screaming, yelling, bullying or becoming violent;
— Planning the death of the alcoholic, seeing it as the only way out.

The more a caretaker tries, the more devious the alcoholic becomes in hiding the drink; the more she tries, the more inadequate and shameful she feels. She thinks she is failing him. She believes that his drinking is somehow her fault, she becomes preoccupied with the problem. She doesn't realise that instead of helping him, she is cushioning him from reality. She is encouraging the development of his denial system and she is pushing him further into the illness.

I have been describing the caretaker as a woman, perhaps a wife or partner. Men, too, can fall into the caretaking role, particularly if he is the husband, boyfriend or father of a female alcoholic. With a young alcoholic, it can be a parent; in other families, the eldest child or eldest daughter can take on that role especially if the non-alcoholic parent is seen as not coping or if both parents are out-of-control drinkers. Indeed, the whole family can consist of several caretakers.

One thing is very clear (to the outsider) that a relationship between a caretaker and alcoholic is not equally balanced. Most of the alcoholic's love is directed towards that tantalizing liquid. It doesn't mean that he doesn't care for his close ones, it means that they are of secondary importance. The further he gets into the illness, the more self-centred he becomes. He comes to be extremely insensitive to their needs — manipulating and lying in order to get to his bottle.

Now and then, outside professional helpers such as social workers, probation officers, nurses, clergymen, alcoholism counsellors, doctors and solicitors can fall into this role of caretaker. This happens because they want to help but don't really understand the nature of alcoholism. Also, perhaps, because they haven't looked honestly at the extent of their need to caretake, as yet. The addiction of professionals to the role of caretaker could be the subject of another book, I believe.

The Difference between Caring and Caretaking

In order to help an alcoholic and his family, it is important to understand the difference between caring and caretaking.

When I was training as a counsellor, it was very strongly suggested I learn to respect my alcoholic clients and believe that they could cope with their own pain. That is caring. What I had been doing was trying to stop them from hurting, believing that they did not have the ability to cope. I was assuming the right to shield and protect them from life's problems. That is caretaking.

A carer has courage and gives the alcoholic the opportunity to get well by letting go of her need to look after him; letting him take the consequences of his drinking behaviour; letting the illness follow its own course, even by letting him get hurt. A caretaker enables him to go further into the illness by making his drinking more comfortable, by shielding him from reality, by treating him like a helpless child. Some of the differences between caretaking and caring behaviour are illustrated in the following table:

A CARETAKER	A CARER
Believes that alcoholic is incapable of dealing with his own problems.	Believes that alcoholic has ability to cope with his problems when sober.
Believes that alcoholic is not strong enough to cope with emotional pain.	Believes that alcoholic has inner strength, but that it has been sapped by the drinking. This strength can be reborn when he achieves abstinence from alcohol.
Protects alcoholic by lying, covering up for him.	Refuses to protect him from police or other family members. Refuses to lie to employer or make excuses for his absences from work.
Tries to control his drinking by bullying, manipulating, bargaining, hiding bottles etc.	Accepts she does not have the power to control his drinking.
Adopts 'no-talking rule'. Is frightened to talk to alcoholic about his drinking in case it upsets him and makes him drink more.	Talks to alcoholic at appropriate time (when sober) about his behaviour under influence of alcohol.

A CARETAKER	A CARER
Devalues herself. Neglects her own needs. Ceases to have a life of her own — becomes an extension to the alcoholic. Is preoccupied by drinker and obsesses about his behaviour. Becomes a martyr.	Values self. Makes sure she has time and space just for herself. Has her own interests. Refuses to be a martyr.
Becomes isolated from others. Doesn't realise she needs help too.	Accepts she cannot cope with living with alcoholism on her own. Seeks help from professionals or self-help groups like Al-Anon.
Represses her feelings. Denies anger because she thinks it is wrong to be angry with someone who is sick.	Recognises and accepts her feelings including anger and depression. Shares them when appropriate.
Blames herself or others for the alcoholic's drinking. Believes the alcoholic when he apportions blame. Allows herself to be manipulated and intimidated by the alcoholic.	Knows that alcoholism is an illness, therefore accepts it is no one's fault. Cannot be manipulated by alcoholic. Refuses to be intimidated.
Thinks that she is the only person who really understands the alcoholic.	Suggests to the alcoholic that he get help from A.A. or a treatment centre.
Hates admitting defeat. Strives over and over again to find the answer that will stop his drinking.	Accepts her limitations. Admits her powerlessness over the drinking.
Spends lots of time and energy being obsessed about the alcoholic. Avoids facing her own emotional pain by doing this.	Shares her feelings of anxiety and fear. Accepts pain and works through it.
Is stuck in the security of known misery. "Better the devil you know."	Has faith that life will get better if she continues to change *her* thoughts and behaviour.

This does not mean to suggest that those who fall into the caretaking role don't care. They do — often, too much.

Many people recognise how they have been enabling the alcoholic further into the illness, as well as noticing how they have been negating their own needs and feelings. As a result they face their fear and pain, get some support from groups like Al-Anon and learn to let go of their alcoholic's problems in a loving way. That is, they hand the responsibility of his illness back to the drinker: supporting all his attempts at recovery but refusing to condone the drinking.

Others find the only way that they can cope is to shut that person out of their lives by disowning or divorcing him. That is the right of the individual. For the sake of her sanity, it is important that she find some stability. However, when the separation is achieved through bitterness or rage, the caretaker rarely finds peace of mind (unless she receives help) and often moves on, seeking another needy person to look after. Many of those that fall into the caretaking role have more than one close relationship with an alcoholic or other type of addict in the process of their lifetime.

Some individuals who read this book will balk at the suggestion that there is really very little we can do to help the alcoholic, other than stand back and let him take responsibility for himself. A few may be very angry and dismiss the writer as crazy, even when they are exhausted or depressed. Others will know in their hearts that this is what they ought to do, even set out to achieve it; yet, almost despite themselves, they keep finding themselves back in that helping role over and over again.

If you fall into categories mentioned in the last two paragraphs, it may be that your greatest problem is not the alcoholic in your life, but yourself. It may be that the alcoholic is in your life because of a need in you; a need to be in the role of caretaker despite the fact that that involvement is causing you pain, stress, depression, perhaps suicidal thoughts. Also, it is important to face your delusion that you are helping the alcoholic by caretaking; it is more likely that you are pushing him further into the illness. It may be that you are addicted to the alcoholic — or addicted to the role you play in your relationship. If so, the term of jargon used in many treatment centres to describe your condition is 'codependence'.

Caretaking and Addictive Love

Perhaps it is important here to define what we mean by the term addiction. It is much more than a habit or repetitive behaviour. It often grows from that. My simple definition of addiction is that it is a compulsive need to use something outside ourselves to stop us from facing our own pain or make us feel good. If you can't control when you start or stop the behaviour, if you are obsessively involved in it, despite the fact that it is damaging your relationships, then you are suffering from addiction. Addiction is also progressive: it gets worse unless it is addressed.

It is easy to see that the alcoholic is addicted. After all, he uses alcohol to make him feel better, and it is obvious that it is unpredictable when he will start or stop drinking. It is also easy to see that his close relationships are suffering as a result of his imbibing.

Addiction to the role of caretaker is much more subtle and not so easy to see. The caretaker can be viewed by herself and others as very noble or generous for loving the alcoholic so much as to tolerate his continuing offensive behaviour. Those who take care of alcoholics can gain a lot of self-esteem from it and as a result can't see caretaking as potentially destructive.

Henry is a good example of someone who is addicted to his caretaking role. His wife is called Victoria. She has been recovering from alcoholism for over two years. Since then, she hasn't touched a drop of alcohol; she has found a new lease of life. She is going to college, attends Alcoholics Anonymous, and as well as receiving help there, she helps a lot of others with the same illness. Her only problem is Henry. Henry doesn't like the new confident, assertive, sober Vicky. He is shocked that he doesn't like her sober, because this is what he hoped and prayed for. Despite his best intentions he is shaken by the depth of his rage and by his continuing desire to put her down and undermine her confidence. He has even been wishing for the old familiar, yet terrible pattern that happened in the drinking days. At least he felt needed then! He is jealous of A.A. and the fact she seemed to get well for them but not for him.

Henry is at a crossroads in his life. He has three choices:

1. To keep on trying to belittle Victoria's attempts at recovery, trying to make her drink and therefore dependent on him again.

2. To continue to deny that the problem is his, putting all the blame for the breakdown of the relationship on his wife. He moves out of the marriage and finds another partner who will be a damsel in distress, feeding his need to be a knight in shining armour. His relationships are centred around power rather than love.

3. To be honest and admit that he has a fundamental personality disorder. He has a compulsive need for a partner who is dependent and in pain. His obsession with trying to 'fix' her is a

way of stopping him facing his grief, his depression, his feeling of inadequacy. In short, he is addicted to Vicky's pain, to her illness. If he wants to change, he needs help. It is difficult to change such an ingrained problem in a short time, on his own. The Al-Anon programme will help him detach from Vicky, with love. Hopefully, through time, Henry and Victoria may rebuild their relationship.

Tragically, addiction to caretaking has a devious and destructive denial system like addiction to alcohol or any other substance. Many careworn codependants (men and women) are blind to the fact that they need to change. They are so hooked into the obsessive belief that if the alcoholic sobered up, everything would be all right. Henry's story is not an isolated one. Many partners 'need' the alcoholic's illness to make them feel good. Numbers hang on, vainly trying to persuade, manipulate, bully, blackmail the alcoholic into stopping drinking. In the process they become embittered, exhausted, depressed, suspicious of others, frightened, isolated. Possibly, they become violent, suicidal or involved in other addictions like alcoholism, dependence on tranquillizers, eating disorders like anorexia, obesity and bulimia. They sacrifice their own lives, believing they have a mission to save that of their alcoholic. They forget that they are mere humans with limitations. They are caught up in a dance with their alcoholic partner which is whirling them both closer and closer to despair, dereliction and possibly death.

Perhaps the extent of the obsessive need to control is illustrated in the words of Sheila. On being told of her alcoholic husband's overdose and subsequent death she bitterly yelled, "The bugger has beaten me!" Words that have been echoed over the years by other partners — partners who have been involved in many exhausting and destructive power struggles — who have striven vainly to try and keep their out-of-control drinker happy, sober and alive.

Characteristics of Someone who is Addicted to Caretaking

I want to stress that not everyone who has a close relationship with an alcoholic is addicted to caretaking. Many are and those who do have that dependency need as much help as the addicted drinker.

However, one of the characteristics of those of us who are caretakers is that we will deny this need for help for ourselves. I will examine more deeply the denial of the caretaker in the next few pages. It is sufficient to say here that most people falling into this category present themselves as copers; independent and strong in character. We are usually solid, responsible people. However, at some time in our lives we reach a point of exhaustion, a point where we are drained, because, although we have been giving out so much, we have not been able to receive. We have not been able to nurture our own needs. If we seek help, it is not usually for ourselves, but to try and find help to fix or control the alcoholic.

Codependent persons will take on far more than 50% of the responsibility, guilt or blame in any relationship. Often, we are convinced that we have somehow brought about the alcoholism. Although it doesn't cause the addiction, what we don't see is that the characteristic we value most in ourselves enables the alcoholic further into his illness. Namely, our overwhelming capacity and drive to care and help.

Many caretakers view that personality trait as our only redeeming quality. In other respects, our self-esteem is minimal. So much emphasis has been put on the tendency to care for others that we have no real sense of who we are. Often, in our family or origin, being responsible, looking after others, putting other people's needs first was the main way we learned to gain other people's approval.

Therefore, in adulthood, we continue that pattern, only feeling lovable when we tend to the requirements of others. Our overpowering need is to be needed. Being terrified of rejection, we do anything to keep the relationship from dissolving. Caretakers tend not to be attracted to stable, reliable people who are interested in them and their needs. Often when we get what we want in a relationship, we become disinterested. The drama of the chase is what excites us.

Because of the compulsive need to take care of others, caretakers unconsciously look for pain or feelings of inadequacy in others. Usually it is the other's hurt that is the attraction rather than the person himself. Searching out other people's pain is a way of stopping us from facing our own.

Codependent people are often lonely and isolated, often feeling that they are loved only for that caretaking part of their personality.

Many times they wish that they hadn't got themselves in the position of being everyone's 'agony aunt', but they don't know how to ask to have their needs met. Usually, although they are very sensitive to other people's feelings, and aware of what other people need to change, they cannot see their own needs.

Obsessive preoccupation with the alcoholic, how he is feeling, what he is up to, is a major characteristic of those of us who are codependent. We spend hours each day or lying awake at night worrying about our situation. We scheme up different techniques to stop the drinking, we rehearse our lectures to the addicted person, anticipating his responses. We torture ourselves worrying where that person is and with whom. We are often aware that this compulsive thinking is doing us no good and we try to stop it but — it won't go away. Sometimes we find we are obsessive about other things, like the cleanliness of the house, or channelling our energy into achieving at work or caretaking someone else, perhaps one of the children.

Obsessive thinking and behaviour does serve a purpose. It helps block out the reality of the situation, the feeling of powerlessness, of impotence. It blocks out the anxiety and fear: the feelings of being isolated and unsupported, the terror of being alone. Obsession is part of the denial of the caretaker. That denial system is as ingrained as that of the alcoholic.

Denial of the Caretaker

One of the reasons that an individual goes so far into his alcoholism before he gets help (or indeed, often never gets help) is because of the covering up in the family. So frequently chaos reigns, many traumatic situations have happened and people have been severely hurt before someone in the family asks for help. Alcoholism is an illness that many believe happens in other families, but not in our own.

A lot of us don't know what alcoholism is. We believe that the drinking binges are only a temporary reaction to stress, and as a result we get hooked into a never-ending game of believing that, "Next time it will be different". Some families put their heads down, close their eyes to reality, grit their teeth and keep on convincing themselves that next time it will be better, because they can't see any other way out of the situation. Somehow, they have got stuck in the security of known misery syndrome and won't, or can't, budge from there. Change might mean a different kind of agony. At least they know and are accustomed to this pain. It has a terrible kind of familiarity and security. Tragically, emotional paralysis has set in.

The problem is that not only are family members denying the extent of the alcoholism, but they are also blind to the reality of how they are involved or how they are affected.

Denial of Powerlessness

The greatest frustration for many caretakers is that all of their efforts to stop the drinking appear to be ineffectual. However, it seems almost impossible for some of us to accept the futility of our efforts. Eagerly, we keep searching for that elusive solution to the problem. How do we stop him or her from drinking? Some of us have to really suffer, to hit some kind of emotional rock bottom before we can accept and admit complete powerlessness over the behaviour of the alcoholic.

Our efforts to control the drinking and crazy actions of the addicted drinker are often an attempt to install some security in our lives. Instead of trying to find that comforting feeling within ourselves, we put all our effort and energy into trying to get the alcoholic to change and provide the stability. Of course, he keeps rocking the boat, keeps letting us down. Obsessively, we keep trying to fix him; tidying him up, lecturing him, covering his tracks, rescuing him from the consequences of his drinking. Hanging on to the omnipotent belief that we have or should have the right and the ability to change another human being. We cannot accept that he does not listen to us, chooses not to hear us; that he prefers to listen to the call of his mistress — alcohol. It is difficult to admit even to ourselves that we don't have the power that we have assumed. Fear stops us from yielding to our powerlessness; from standing back and letting go. To admit the truth is to feel the pain, the depression, the grief of being powerless.

Denial of Feelings

A caretaker is no longer an individual person in her own right. She has become an extension of the alcoholic. Most of her thoughts, her actions, her energy, revolves around what the alcoholic is doing. She suppresses her needs as a human being; her priority, as she sees it, is her need to fix the alcoholic. In her drive to achieve some kind of stability, she sweeps aside her own feelings.

High stress and lack of predictability are part of the environment for the family living with an alcoholic. Most of those concerned try to avoid depression and anxiety by attempting to control the drinker. Feelings are treated as a nuisance factor, as something which may rock the boat. The family tiptoes around the alcoholic as though on eggshells, pretending that everything is alright.

In her effort to present herself as a coper, the caretaker will smile sweetly at the world, conning herself and most other people into believing that everything is just fine with her. Inside, deep down, she is a steaming cauldron of emotions. Most caretakers will look highly indignant at the suggestion they might be angry. "How can I possibly be angry with someone who is as sick and helpless as the alcoholic?" To take this attitude is to deny the traumatic effect of living with the constant tension, worries, deceit, put-downs: the never-knowing what to expect next, the playing one family member off against another. I believe it's impossible to live in a situation like that and not be angry. Also, a caretaker is often angry because she has fantasies of what her relationship with the alcoholic 'should' be, and it never meets that expectation. The grief of unfulfilled dreams is painful.

Focussing on the pain of the alcoholic is a way of preventing her from standing still and facing her own. The warm sympathy, the cool composure of many caretakers hides the deep wounds of shame, guilt, low self-esteem, grief, depression and fear. Often those raw feelings are just below the surface, but a typical caretaker is frightened to admit them because it may mean that for a time she will lose control, and that is what she is desperately hanging onto.

Denial of Reality

Sometimes, in order to shut off their feelings, those who caretake alcoholics have to close the door on reality. For example, my colleagues and I have heard many horrific tales of damage to families from alcoholics who are just beginning to break down their denial system. Yet, when we have met with those relatives, they have been insistent that, "Things have not been that bad really". When reminded of embarrassing or violent incidents, many family members genuinely can't remember, or they have pushed it so far back in their memories that to bring it to the surface causes much distress and anguish. There are so many layers of stress accumulated over the years living with an alcoholic. Sometimes the only way to cope is to pretend even to oneself that it didn't happen.

Another area of reality that relatives can deny is the effect of the drinking and of their obsessive caretaking on the children. As I will explain in other chapters, the young people are the most forgotten, most ignored. So many parents, alcoholic and non-alcoholic, are adamant that their children do not know anything about the drinking or have not been adversely affected by it. Yet, in my experience they are the most aware and sadly, in most cases, they will have been harmed by the consequences of alcoholism. On the surface, they can look so good, so put-together, just like their caretaker parent. So often, like their caretaking parent they have learned not to rock the boat, to deny the reality of themselves. They, too, are repressing feelings of inadequacy, guilt, shame, anger and fear. Usually, they have no one to talk to, because both parents are too preoccupied with their respective addictions. To talk outside the family is often seen as disloyal. Thus, they are denied any kind of support which they desperately need.

Denial of Need for Help

On learning about a new book, a new treatment programme, a new way to try and control or stop the alcoholic's drinking, most caretakers will be right there, eager to learn. This, despite the fact that the addicted drinker does not want to know. On the other hand, suggest to a caretaker that she needs some help and she will look at you in amazement. She may be depressed, exhausted, burnt out; she may have no life of her own outside her fixation with the alcoholic; she may not be able to shut out that obsessive voice in her head. Still, she insists that she doesn't have a problem. After all, she isn't drinking a bottle of whisky a day; she is coping with a full-time job, two children and an out-of-control drinker. Stop the alcoholic from drinking and all her problems will be over!

Unfortunately, she may find that if the alcoholic recovers, she has been scapegoating him. Like Henry, she may find that the drinker's recovery does not bring instant happiness. She may discover she has a lot of adjusting to do. Some caretakers may find letting go of that role extremely frightening and difficult.

The alcoholic may need help, but equally, so does the caretaker. Sometimes, recovery from codependence is even more difficult than recovery from alcoholism. The latter starts with abstaining from alcohol. Human beings cannot abstain from relationships; we need them to survive. Healing from the caretaking addiction means we have to change the way we relate to others. That may mean changing a pattern of survival that we have learned from childhood.

Part III

Freedom from Addiction

5

Detaching with Love

"It isn't easy to admit defeat, when I've tried so hard to handle my problems in my own way. But I do know that I cannot move forward unless I am willing to stop trying to control others and their compulsions."

Twelve Steps and Twelve Traditions, Al-Anon

This is the chapter on how to help the alcoholic. Possibly a number of caretakers are not going to be too happy with the advice given, because the main emphasis is *not* on how the out-of-control drinker can change but how *you*, the family member, can. Others may be relieved to find some solution to the problem. The best way you can help your alcoholic, your children, and other relatives who may be enmeshed in the protective system that the family provides is to get help for *yourself*. Alcoholism is not among the problems you can solve; your anxiety, depression, obsessive thinking and fear are.

At the back of the book you will find the telephone number and address of Al-Anon headquarters. They will advise you on the whereabouts of your local meeting. Al-Anon is a self-help group which is designed to help relatives of an alcoholic. There are no professionals involved, only people who are living with or have lived with a drinking alcoholic. Everyone helps each other let go of their obsessive preoccupation with their alcoholic. The programme is designed to help friends and family detach from the alcoholic — with love. That means giving up, or greatly diminishing, the role of caretaker.

Please note, 'letting go' of the alcoholic does not necessarily mean that you have to leave him. It would be wise to protect yourself and the children by moving out, if he has become violent, or alternatively, arranging for him to move out. However, the threat of leaving, and sometimes actually doing that, are quite often manipulative moves on the part of the caretaker to try and stop the drinking. Sometimes it works for a short time and then the old game of, "Who is going to win this time?", starts all over again. Nevertheless, many families do reach a stage when they can tolerate no more pain and have the right to choose to move away from its source.

The kindest gesture you can make towards your alcoholic is to give him back his rights. That is, the right to drink if he chooses to, the right to make mistakes, the right to get hurt and the right to make a choice on whether he recovers or not.

For someone who has grimly hung on to the role of caretaker for years, deciding to give it up sometimes produces a similar sensation to that of jumping off a cliff. Fear and panic can be overwhelming. Detaching with love is not something that is accomplished instantly. Many caretakers have a drive to achieve, a need to be seen as successful. The dangers are to expect too much too soon or to set unrealistically high goals. Healing from the ravages of addiction has to be seen as a process which takes time. It is important to be gentle and patient with oneself, to share the pain with someone who is travelling on a similar pathway of growth.

One thing is certain: initially, the alcoholic will not appreciate the change in you! He has lost his mother figure (whether you are male or female) who has been taking responsibility for his behaviour; as well as this, his nagging scapegoat has disappeared, leaving him without that wonderful justification for his drinking! It is likely that he will try and make you feel guilty for being different. His drinking may even get worse for a while. He will do his best to get you hooked onto the old, repetitive games. With the help of Al-Anon, you will be able to stand back from his manipulations and let him take responsibility for himself. It is like changing the steps of an exhausting and difficult dance. You can step back from the out-of-control whirling of your partner and choose to move at your own rhythm with your own unique steps.

Reducing the Obsessive Thinking

When a human being is continually and obsessively preoccupied by something or someone outside himself, he is actually struggling to find a way to meet an unfulfilled inner need. This applies to the compulsive overeater who can't get home quickly enough to devour the contents of her fridge. It is also demonstrated by the alcoholic who puts the people he loves second to his need for the bottle; or by the gambler who loses the family's hard earned housekeeping money on a 'flutter' in a vain attempt to find that high from winning; or by the drug addict who sells his mother's jewellery in order to buy a 'fix'. Equally, but perhaps not so obviously, it is exhibited by the typical behaviour of a caretaker who spends hours scheming up different methods of controlling her alcoholic.

Obsession is a process often used to try and solve problems. The ever-circling preoccupation with thoughts, manipulations and plans of action helps the family member feel she is doing something to help. Also, it temporarily helps block out some of the anxiety and fear; but it is not a solution. Many caretakers cut off their creativity and waste valuable time by rehearsing what they are going to say next, going over painful events from the past or fretting over the whereabouts of the alcoholic's most recent hidey-hole.

Compulsive worrying and the overpowering flooding of one's mind can be gradually reduced by shifting the focus of attention off the alcoholic and on to one's own needs. This can be done by sharing concerns and feelings with others and by developing a 'sense of self' as described later in this chapter. It also requires allowing space and time to work through the following course of events.

The Grieving Process

The decision to drop the role of caretaker means the end of one or more relationships. It may be that the dependent relationship is gradually being replaced by a healthier new one with the same person. However, the role of caretaker is one that has taken up most of our time, most of our energy, most of our thoughts, and most of our feelings. Giving it up produces an overpowering sense of loss. As with other major losses in our lives, in order to adjust to it, we have to go through a period of grief.

There are several stages in the grieving process that we have to move through before we can find the serenity of acceptance. We don't necessarily work through the process in the order shown here. Usually, we weave backwards and forwards between the stages. It can take months to come through it. We may find that as we face the loss, it may arouse feelings of grief for past bereavements. In their efforts to cope, most caretakers have gone through their lives avoiding pain or not letting it take the natural course of working itself out. Facing one set of grief can unlock others.

I believe that this is a time when caretakers cannot depend on their own strength of character to see them through. It is a time to be vulnerable, to ask for help from others; a time to be with people who understand, accept and love them for who they are. Their alcoholic, whether he is drinking or in early recovery, is not going to be the person who will provide that support. He is too wrapped up in his own problems and, at this time, is too insensitive to the needs of others.

Denial

If the addicted caretaker is to change and let go, she must, at some stage, face the reality that her problem is not the alcoholic but her voracious need to be needed; as well as her fear of abandonment and the illusion of having the power to control others. Quite often, it is only when a codependent person has been backed into a corner or hurt enough that she will face her denial system and accept the need for change within herself. The fantasy that if he will stop drinking, everything will be wonderful, finally runs its course and breaks down. The feelings that have been repressed or suppressed fight their way to the surface and demand to be recognised. The pain forces her into a decision of facing the truth or continuing to opt out of taking responsibility for her life and the need to change its direction. Sometimes the pain and depression are so deep, the decision can be between choosing to live and choosing to die.

Like the alcoholic, the caretaker is not going to change until she is ready for it. Perhaps, like her partner, she has to experience the extreme pain of her addiction before she can make that decision. She too has to hit an emotional rock bottom.

Anger

Facing reality brings a lot of rage with it. When a caretaker starts to come through the fog of denial, she can find she is angry at so many things. Angry at her alcoholic for continuing to drink: "If he loved me he would stop". Angry at herself for being powerless to change his problem; angry at the 'wasted' years; angry at having to be the one to change, perhaps; angry at other people for not understanding. Maybe, also, she is angry at God, if she believes in Him, for putting her in this situation: "What have I done to deserve this?"

Rage can be frightening for someone who has invested so much of her life in appearing cool and put together. Many will try to diminish the intensity of the feeling by using milder euphemisms such as disappointment, cross or upset. However, the truth is usually that there are layers of repressed anger struggling to burst out. It is important that the recovering caretaker has someone to talk to; to share those feelings with someone who understands, perhaps a friend in Al-Anon. So much can be lost if that person is told that she shouldn't be angry at the alcoholic because he is sick. That is what she has been telling herself for years and that is one of the reasons why she is stuck.

Thinking about it, how is it possible to live with the constant belittling comments, the deceit, the lies, the disappearing of the alcoholic, the playing one family member off against another and not be angry? The tension, the never knowing what to expect next, the fear, the worry, the blaming, the isolation, all contribute to that powerful build up of rage. Pushing it down or denying the feeling just encourages it to fester and eventually explode. It is possible to learn to deal with it in a healthier, more constructive way.

Anger can be a positive drive. It can help the codependent person start to move and commence fighting constructively for her rights and her needs. It can be a creative force which can help her find her rightful way in life. It can be liberating when channelled in the right direction. Talking to someone outside the family, in a safe environment, helps take the edge off the intensity of the feeling. Hopefully, this prevents her from getting into the old, destructive goading of the alcoholic which hurts them both. Thumping cushions, physical exercise, expressing anger on paper by writing about it or drawing it, and possibly tearing it up are other ways of channelling that pent up energy.

It isn't necessary and it really serves no purpose to continually dump the rage on the out-of-control drinker. Chances are that he will use it as a justification to go on a drinking binge, feeling incensed or self-piteous because his partner has become so out of control!

Bargaining

As I mentioned before, most family members or friends will seek help so that they can find ways to stop their alcoholic's drinking. Al-Anon is full of people who have gone along to meetings just for that purpose. It has taken months, sometimes years for the penny to drop; to come to believe that liberation is actually found in changing oneself — not the alcoholic. When that message is absorbed, unless one has really understood it and achieved an inner peace, it is very easy and quite usual to fall into the trap of making adjustments immediately, but with the wrong motives. The slogan "Let go and let God", has not been fully comprehended. The attitude is, "I understand what you mean by detaching with love and I want to be able to do it but — are you really sure there is *nothing* I can do to stop him from drinking? How will I feel if I let go and he dies or goes to jail? How will I live with myself?" This person wants to let go, has perhaps even tried to do it, but she is still hanging on to her illusion of power. She still believes that she should have the right and the ability to keep her loved one alive. She is still placing herself in a god-like position. She is using the concept of 'letting go' as yet another manipulation to try and change her partner.

Depression

This is a time of pain, of feeling hopeless and helpless, of wondering, "What is the point?" Most people who let go of the role of caretaker and detach with love appear to have to go through this before they really surrender and accept their powerlessness over others. Many will try and avoid the pain. Most codependants, although experts at sensing the agony of others, are not good at standing still and facing their own. Perhaps because we live in a society which subtly implies that if we feel pain or depression we've done something wrong. For some people the feeling of suffering is correlated with admitting failure. Sadly, they cannot see it as a time of human growth, and they stunt their potential as human beings, locked into the denial of feelings.

Some of the depression arises from questions like, "Who am I? After all these years of putting massive amounts of effort into looking good, sensing other people's problems and taking care of them: take that away from me or ask me to reduce my mothering role and what am I left with? I've lived my life trying to please other people and now realise I have been untrue to myself. What are my values? What do I need? How do I learn to like myself? What are my feelings? Will people like me if I am no longer caretaking? Will I be abandoned — left on my own? If so, how will I cope?"

Sometimes the pain of loss is like being in a big black hole. The only way out is to acknowledge it, feel it and let the emotion pass in its own time. Talking with a friend or therapist provides support during this process and helps reduce the feeling of intense loneliness. This is a time when the caretaker really needs help from others. Sometimes the blackness is overwhelming. Fighting it, saying it shouldn't be happening, or "I ought to be coping better than this", seems to give the feeling more power. Surrendering and accepting that it's going to hurt for a while seems to make it more tolerable and eventually the suffering diminishes.

It is very important that the sufferers be gentle with themselves at this time and not indulge in self-blame. Every caretaker has an intention that is good and reasonable; that is, to help someone else and feel better themselves. They survive, help and care in the best way they know how: the way many of us have been taught by previous generations, that to love is to caretake and self deny. Sadly, in both alcoholic and many other relationships it doesn't work. However, many caretakers are beginning to find a way that does — by taking care of themselves first and others second.

Acceptance

Acceptance is a sense of inner peace that is reached very gradually. It is the surrender to *knowing* that we are powerless over the lives of others, no matter how much we love them or how sick they are. It is a liberation, a freeing of the caretaker and the alcoholic to follow whatever path in life they choose. It is the recognition that it is impossible to stand guard over someone else without losing one's own freedom.

To admit powerlessness is to surrender to living life in a new way. It is finding the Freedom to Be — a freedom from the trap of living out one's life as a perplexed and embittered extension of the alcoholic. It is an acceptance that if we love ourselves first we remove ourselves from the constraints of manipulating and controlling. We are free to love and be loved for who we are — not for what we or others think we ought to be.

Valuing the Self

In order to achieve that surrender or acceptance, it is important that the family member or friend achieve a true 'sense of self'. That means the priority is no longer reacting or responding in a way that will please the alcoholic or others; it is assuming responsibility for one's self. It is giving emphasis to accepting accountability for how one feels, what one thinks and how one acts within the family. Having a 'sense of self' means taking time out in a situation to value one's own needs and feelings and consequently make appropriate decisions. It helps one develop a feeling of wholeness and a sense of individuality. It means being who one is — not acting out a role.

So often a codependent person will blame others, particularly the alcoholic, for the way he or she feels or what he or she does. Statements are made like, "I wouldn't nag if you didn't drink so much", or "You make me so angry", or "If only she would stop drinking then my life would get back to normal". Statements which stop the family member from taking responsibility for his or her own behaviour. Statements which trap the speaker into waiting in vain for other people to change so that life will get better.

Finding that 'sense of self' means you can believe that no one else is able to upset you unless you choose to let it happen. It means you have a choice in how you respond to your alcoholic when he continues to belittle you. You can choose to be on the defensive and attack back — or not. You can choose to believe his taunts — or you can choose to trust your own feelings, instincts or intuition. You can be free to be calm when he is trying to provoke you into being upset. You can have the confidence to say 'no' when you're uncomfortable with saying 'yes'.

In short, finding a 'sense of self' means learning to value and love oneself. We can avoid so many of the painful struggles in relationships by developing, strengthening and validating the self. When we are at peace with ourselves we do not fear abandonment so much. We do not run from intimacy.

When we value our own selves, it is easier to ratify the individuality of the self in those close to us. We believe that everyone including ourselves has the right to express anger, fear, hurt and loneliness. We can support others in doing so, without taking away their sense of self by taking on the responsibility of their feelings or wanting to absorb their pain.

Here is a list of behaviours of people who have learned to value their 'sense of self'. This list is an ideal, a goal to work towards. No one achieves all of this all of the time, nor should expect themselves to.

— They feel good about themselves and comfortably accept compliments or gifts.

— They set aside time and space for themselves when they can relax and do what pleases them. They are not afraid of being alone. They enjoy their own company. They learn to say 'no' and not overcommit themselves.

— They do not assume that they are the only people who can take care of problems. They recognise their own needs, ask for help and allow themselves to be taken care of. They learn to balance 50% giving with 50% receiving. They feel free to express their fear and loneliness.

— They do not over-react to others' aggression or belittling. They learn to express anger assertively and effectively. Having expressed it they don't hang on to the resentment. They forgive the person and let go.

— They allow themselves to grieve for the loss of a dream of what the relationship could be without the alcoholism. They accept pain as a part of growth.

— They emerge from living in a fantasy world and put some of their dreams into practice.

— They have fun.

— They forgive themselves for making mistakes.

— They set realistic goals and do not try to achieve too much too soon. They learn to trust the process of recovery and accept that growth, healing, redemption, forgiveness and reconciliation all take time.

— They relax from pronouncing judgements on others as well as themselves, becoming less rigid in seeing behaviours as right or wrong and black or white.

— They learn to trust and value their instincts, intuitions and feelings more. They cease to look to others to determine how they should feel.

— They can love unconditionally. They no longer give in order to get.

— They take responsibility for who they are, look at the different ways they can behave in a situation and do what feels right for them.

— They live in the present day, confident that they can cope with what that space of time can offer them. No longer do they need to worry about the future or feel guilty about the past.

— They learn to place themselves with positive people who value and respect the self, whose eyes light up when they see them. On the other hand, they cut down the amount of time they spend with people who are negative, who try to diminish the sense of self. This may include the alcoholic.

— They seek and welcome intimacy in trusting relationships.

— Many come to value the self by experiencing a relationship with a caring God or Higher Power. This does not necessarily mean being involved in organised religion, but believing in a positive spiritual influence. A sense of Goodness which positively affects our lives if we let go of fear, of trying to control life's direction.

As a result of having this outlook these people *know* the difference between 'detaching with love' and exercising the need to control another. They are free to live out their own destiny.

How does Detaching with Love Help the Alcoholic?

As well as releasing the caretaker so that she can live her own life, detaching with love helps free the alcoholic to experience his own crises: crises produced by his drinking behaviour. Many addicted drinkers have been so protected from reality by their next of kin that, (coupled with the denial system of alcoholism) they genuinely believe that their drinking is not that bad. However, when spouses and other family members get help in regaining their own emotional health they often precipitate crises for the alcoholic without even being aware of it. Besides the fact they no longer rescue him from the results of his drinking escapades, their new attitudes and behaviour put more pressure on the alcoholic. In effect, their healthiness makes his drinking too uncomfortable for him.

So many recovering alcoholics report that it was their partner's detachment from their drinking behaviour that eventually led them to enter treatment. They felt so threatened by the caretaker's standing back that they felt the need to seek help. This, after years of ignoring the family's pleas, nagging, bullying and manipulating. Other alcoholics have stated that they felt great fear because their families had got on with enjoying a full life without them. The addicted drinkers felt left out. Eventually, that feeling of isolation was the thing that pushed them into desiring recovery.

In short, caretakers who seek help and support for themselves, who achieve a 'sense of self' and a stabilisation of their emotional health are better able to help the alcoholic. By helping themselves, they automatically help the drinker because they are more able to let go and allow the alcoholic to experience his own crises and pain.

These can be some of the effects that learning to detach with love can have on the alcoholic. Let's look at some others in more detail.

The Effect of Not Rescuing the Alcoholic

When a family member finally accepts her powerlessness over the alcoholic's drinking and gives him back the right to be responsible for his own life, she starts to make some changes in the way she relates to him. One of the first things she does is to choose not to rescue him from the messes that his drinking gets him into. She can do this in several ways — by not paying his debts; by not making excuses to his boss for his absences at work; by not picking him up, dusting him down, dragging him upstairs and tucking him in bed when he falls over drunk; by leaving evidence of his destructive behaviour where he left it. This may mean leaving the broken Christmas tree and presents so that he can see them sober — where he knocked them over in a drunken stupor. Not rescuing may mean not lying to the children because he has forgotten to take them fishing again; it may mean telling them that he is on another drinking binge. It may mean letting him accept the consequences of drinking and driving. If he insists, for the safety of others as well as himself, it may mean advising the police that he is a hazard on the road.

The message that the caretaker is giving is, "I am no longer accepting responsibility for your drinking, your drinking behaviour, or the consequences of your drinking behaviour. I am giving that responsibility back to you."

Probably the alcoholic will not believe it at first and will try to manipulate his way out of the situation. By this time, as the truth of his drinking slowly seeps through, it is likely that he hates himself. One of the ways of avoiding the reality of his self-loathing is to project what he feels about himself on to others. Usually he does this unconsciously, but his superior attitude is an attempt to make him feel better. He masks his self-disgust by grandiose and defiant attacks on his partner. He sees others as 'spiteful', 'against him' or 'inferior'. Detaching with love may well be seen by the alcoholic as total rejection. He senses that he is losing control of his family's need to feel responsible for him and he tries to make them feel guilty for daring to unhook themselves. If his partner is receiving professional help, or involved in Al-Anon and becoming emotionally more healthy herself, he may describe her as 'neurotic' and give a similar label to her friends. He sees the whole world as conspiring against him. His addicted mind prefers to believe this rather than accept his drinking is the problem.

It is important to remember that the alcoholic is not likely to get well if his drinking is still giving him a lot of pleasure. It is only when it gets uncomfortable or painful that he will recognise the need to give it up. Sometimes that process can seem incredibly slow. It takes a lot of patience, and a lot of love from families as they work through this sequence of events. For a while the drinking, aggression and belittling comments may get worse as he hurts more. Friends who understand the situation are very important to family members at this time; friends who will support the decision to continue 'detaching with love'. Friends who don't understand, who try to persuade you that what you are doing to your alcoholic is cruel, are not what you need at the moment. Perhaps you need to detach from them, too, for a while.

The Effects of Not Responding to the Manipulations of the Alcoholic

When a caretaker has taken time to work on improving her own emotional health, her self esteem greatly increases. She is able to stand her ground, and she does not need the approval of others to confirm what feels right for her. Equally, she is not easily 'put-down' by the alcoholic's belittling comments. Neither does she need his dependence to encourage her to feel good about herself. She has found ways within her own personality and by developing her own creativity which enhance her feelings of self worth. She has become centred within herself.

Previously, because the centre of her life was focussed on the alcoholic, he had a tremendous amount of power over her. Her moods and her feelings depended on his moods and his feelings. Her decisions were made after she considered the state of his drinking and the state of his mind. Her needs had become secondary to his needs.

Now that she has achieved a 'sense of self' she knows that he does not have the power to upset her unless she lets it happen. Also, she has probably taken time to learn about alcoholism and she knows it is an illness and therefore not her fault. As she becomes less isolated and involves herself with others, she knows she is liked and accepted for who she is. The alcoholic's taunts which accuse her of being neurotic, crazy, lazy, or 'being a slob' no longer have such an intense effect.

Gradually, the alcoholic becomes aware that he is losing the ally who unknowingly colluded in his destructive game. This adds to his fear and self-loathing as reality pushes its way through his very solid denial system.

The Effects of Not Nagging or Bullying

The more a family member or friend is able to detach with love, the more frantic the alcoholic becomes, the more he clings to his old delusions of being the only one who is all right; it is everyone else who is out of step. However, the recovering caretaker's behaviour is even beginning to make him doubt that.

Once upon a time, he was able to manipulate reasons for his drinking by setting up an argument with his wife, mother or girlfriend. She would always respond by flying off the handle or nagging for hours about his insensitivity, his neglect of the family or his drinking. He was able to make a good exit, slamming the door and charging down to the pub. Afterwards he could always justify, "See what you made me do! If you didn't nag or weren't such a bully, I wouldn't get so upset and wouldn't need to drink!"

Even that is changing because she won't rise to the bait. She doesn't argue, she doesn't get so out of control with her anger, she doesn't nag and she doesn't bully. The alcoholic is getting more and more uncomfortable because he can no longer scapegoat his partner. That means he has to start looking at himself when he knows his self-disgust is causing him great discomfort and even stronger urges to drink and drown those feelings.

The Effects of Breaking the 'No-Talking Rule'

Even though it is done with the best of intentions, the biggest and most common mistake made by the alcoholic's nearest and dearest is the decision to not talk about the drinking and its consequences. The results of this unspoken rule is the encouragement of the alcoholic's delusion in believing that his drinking is not that bad really.

If they want to help the alcoholic, recovering caretakers learn that they have to talk about their concerns about his dependence on alcohol — to the person who has the problem. Obviously, the alcoholic has to be reasonably sober to hear this. There is no point discussing it while he is drunk. He won't remember. Also he is more likely to hear you if you are calm and matter of fact. Perhaps you could tell him that you are concerned that his drinking has become out of control, giving him specific examples of when you have observed that happening. You may also share with him that you have been seeking help for yourself, so that you can learn to deal with your own problems, and thus cope with his drinking more adequately. It may be appropriate to tell him that he may have an illness, that he could seek advice on this and receive help. If he has the illness of alcoholism, there is treatment available.

It is also important, I believe, to break the 'no-talking rule' with other family members and close trusted friends. This is partly because they might need some help and support themselves in dealing with the drinking problem. This includes children as well as adults. You may be able to recommend Al-Anon or Alateen or encourage them to seek professional help. It may also be important to share with them why you have taken a new attitude to the alcoholic. If they can share their concerns with him in an uncontrolling way, the alcoholic may eventually be prepared to listen.

The alcoholic is very sick and very scared; he believes he has everything under control, or soon will have. He is extremely irrational and it is unlikely that he will get well by having a wonderful, sudden, spontaneous insight of his own. His denial is too strong for that. He needs help from others to break through that barrier and this can only be done with a lot of love, a lot of patience and a lot of talking openly about the reality of his drinking problem. It may be that the family needs to deliver an ultimatum in order to get him into treatment. It may be that his relatives have reached the end of their tether and have to say, "If you want us to stay together as a family then you must change, you must seek treatment".

Considering the Risks of Detaching with Love

In my experience, learning to 'detach with love' is the most effective way of both helping the alcoholic and helping the rest of the family be more stabilized emotionally. However, there is no 100% foolproof guarantee that everyone will live happily ever after. Some families find recovery and peace of mind only to discover that the alcoholic moves away to form a relationship with another caretaker who will protect him from facing reality.

Of course, the other major factor to consider is that death is always imminent with a drinking alcoholic, whether he is in the bosom of his family or not. Often, unknowingly, he is playing a tantalising game of Russian Roulette with alcohol. 'Detaching with love' does not provide a surety that your alcoholic won't die as a result of his drinking, but it does increase his chances of recovery.

Alongside that, 'detaching with love' improves the health, the sense of well-being of the caretaker. If there are children in the family they can only benefit from having one stable, healthy parent.

Detaching with love is not easy; at times, it is an extremely tough love. Nevertheless, it does have many rewards. Detaching with love comes with accepting that love is not ours to use to control or satisfy our ego desires.

> After a while you learn the subtle difference
> Between holding a hand and chaining a soul,
> And you learn that love doesn't mean leaning
> And company doesn't mean security
> And you begin to learn that kisses aren't contracts
> And presents aren't promises,
> And you begin to accept your defeats
> With your head held up and your eyes open,
> With the grace of a woman, not the grief of a child,
> And you learn to build all your roads
> On today because tomorrow's ground
> Is too uncertain for plans, and futures have
> A way of falling down in mid-flight.
> After awhile you learn that even sunshine
> Burns if you get too much.
> So you plant your own garden and decorate
> Your own soul, instead of waiting
> For someone to bring you flowers,
> And you learn that you really can endure...
> That you really are strong
> That you really have worth.
> And you learn and learn...
> With every goodbye you learn.
>
> *Comes the Dawn*, Kara di Giovanne

6

Living without Alcohol

"We admitted we were powerless over alcohol — that our lives had become unmanageable."
Step One of the Twelve Steps and Twelve Traditions of Alcoholics Anonymous

Recovery from alcoholism takes a long time. Many people assume that all the alcoholic has to do is put the cork in the bottle and stop drinking. Indeed, that *is* the beginning, but healing from the ravages of alcoholism is a process rather than an event; possibly a process which takes a lifetime. Not only does the body have to heal from the physical effects of drinking large quantities of alcohol but, the problem drinker has to find a way to cease drinking and stay stopped.

Please note, I will be using the term 'recovering alcoholic' not 'recovered alcoholic'. That is deliberate. There is no known cure for alcoholism, but the disease can be arrested. People with this illness can learn to live a normal, healthy lifestyle as long as they abstain from drinking alcohol. However, the potential for relapse is ever-present, apparently throughout the alcoholic's life-span. Inevitably if this happens, they resume their dependence on alcohol where they left off and it takes over the control of their lives again. Recovery is a way of life that has to be worked at constantly. An alcoholic cannot afford to be complacent or believe that he has the addiction beaten. Hence my use of the adjective 'recovering' rather than 'recovered'. It gives no illusion of false hope, since it illustrates the progressive nature of getting well.

Recovering from alcoholism means learning to accept that one is not responsible for developing the illness, but paradoxically, once it is acknowledged by the sufferer that he is indeed alcoholic, then he has to be accountable for his behaviour. It is also his responsibility to maintain his recovery from alcoholism — with support from others.

Accepting the Inability to Control Alcohol

Many alcoholics avoid or delay recovery because they are unaware that they have an illness from which they can get well. They have been told by themselves or by other people that all they have to do is pull themselves together and cut down the amount they drink or cut it out altogether. Perhaps for days, or weeks, or months, or even years, they have managed to do this, but then the urge to drink becomes so overpowering that they find themselves hooked back into the same old destructive drinking pattern. So many alcoholics view themselves as 'bad' or 'weak' and can't see a way out of the complicated maze of their addiction.

Others will look for all sorts of reasons to explain why their lives are such a mess, convincing themselves that alcohol is not really the problem. They may spend a great deal of time at the doctor's surgery vainly trying to find some serious physical ailment to explain the feeling of inertia. Of course, they don't mention the drinking or if they do, they greatly minimize it. They may take hours trying to find the major problem areas in their lives, believing that if they discovered what these might be, the obsession with alcohol would diminish and they might learn to drink in a 'normal' fashion. They might resolve that it is their jobs, their group of friends, their families or the country they live in that is causing the problem. They may decide to move away and get rid of these components of their lives, usually to find the out-of-control drinking continues.

What the alcoholic is not facing is the fact that he is powerless over alcohol — that he is not in control of it. It has control over him and it is destroying his life. He is psychologically and physically dependent on the drug ethyl alcohol. He has the urge to become intoxicated by that drug. It is an impulse that keeps repeating itself and supercedes all his other needs. It may not be evident all the time. The alcoholic may not think of drink all day, most days or even drink every day; but that urge is there just below the surface and can pop up at any time. Although it can rise up when the alcoholic is stressed, it is, in fact, independent of that feeling. What is more, when he gives in to the drive to drink, he cannot predict what the outcome will be. He doesn't know how much alcohol he will consume, when he will stop drinking, or how he will behave when he is under the influence.

Unless the alcoholic faces, admits, comes to terms with and accepts that he is powerless over alcohol, he is not going to get well. Understanding what is meant by powerlessness is the first step and forms the foundation of recovery. The deeper his understanding and acceptance, the stronger the foundation and thus it is more likely that his addiction will be arrested. However, it isn't easy to admit and surrender to the fact that one cannot control alcohol. Our society is geared towards the approval of success and achievements. Generally, we do not easily accept our limitations as human beings; many are frightened to do so. Those who do not understand the illness judge and condemn alcoholics as failures. Also, as well as coming to terms with the fact that they cannot control alcohol, that it has a destructive force in their lives, as well as the lives of those close to them, alcoholics have to accept that they have to give up what they considered their best friend; their mainstay and the centre of their lives.

Breaking through the Delusion

To accept the concept of powerlessness requires that the alcoholic faces the reality of the destructiveness of his illness; that can be extremely painful. In early recovery, addicted people are not very good at coping with hurt feelings, because they have been anaesthetizing them for years. Many have a low threshold for tolerating pain. It is important that the recoverer has the support of people who understand, who identify with the behaviour, guilt and shame as well as supporting the need to face the truth. This non-judgemental attitude can be found in the self-help group of Alcoholics Anonymous and treatment centres which support the philosophy that recovery from alcoholism begins with total abstinence from alcohol and other mood-altering drugs. People who try and prevent the alcoholic from facing the pain of reality, hinder — not help — his recovery.

Surrending to the fact that one is powerless over the chemical is very rarely a single snap decision. It is usually a sequence of remembering and feeling the reality of several incidents of being out of control while under the influence of that drug. Many treatment centres which support the philosophy mentioned above, place the major emphasis of treatment on confronting the reality of that powerlessness and the damage the drinking has caused to the alcoholic and those close to him. Personality defects and problems in living cannot be realistically dealt with while most of the alcoholic's energy is channelled into maintaining his powerful delusion or his obsession with alcohol.

Gradually, over time, the recovering alcoholic will face the devastating effects of his illness. For example, as he becomes more honest he will see more clearly

— that he cannot control the overwhelming urge to drink
— that he is damaging his health
— that his family and friends have suffered greatly
— that his work has been ineffective
— that there are long periods of time he cannot remember
— that his thinking has become obsessive and deluded
— that his feelings have been denied
— that financially his drinking has drained him
— that he has been behaving in a way that was opposed to his values

Drinking alcoholics are trapped. They aren't living a life, they are merely existing or reduced to fighting for survival. Only through abstinence, along with an understanding and acceptance of their powerlessness will they find a way to freedom — to be the human being they are meant to be. Gradually, as a result of this knowledge, they will release themselves from a life of delusion, from overpowering self-loathing, from the morning shakes, from causing a great deal of family chaos. They will give themselves the opportunity to restore the health of their bodies. The nervous system will no longer be abused, the deterioration of the liver and other vital organs will be stopped. The chance to live a longer life increases.

One of the most healing factors in the alcoholic's recovery is the disintegration of the 'no-talking rule'. For the purpose of becoming open to the acceptance of reality, the addicted drinker needs to share what being out of control has been like for him. Also, in order to jog his memory, it helps to listen to others; he needs to be aware of what his alcoholism was like for his family and close friends and to hear other alcoholics share their experiences. Knowing that others have instigated and lived through similar damaging situations helps ease the guilt, shame and isolation. At the same time, it reminds him of times that his mind has blanked out.

Often, it is a slow, meandering process as the alcoholic comes to accept that his addiction has directly affected every area of his life. Not only has his health been damaged, his family deeply hurt, but his job has suffered through loss of concentration, lost hours and shirked responsibilities. Also, his emotions and behaviours have become greatly distorted and out of control.

Early Recovery

Recovery from alcoholism is an exploration, it is a process of discovering who one is. It can be an adventure; a journey searching for a sense of wholeness. In the early days, it is the beginning of an awareness. The development of one's own thoughts and beliefs, the finding of one's values and the surfacing of one's feelings. Like his partner, the alcoholic has to learn to develop a 'sense of self'. Recovery is about learning to live with oneself and learning to value the uniqueness and creativity of that self.

Possibly it is difficult for many non-dependent drinkers to understand but, alcoholics in early recovery do not know themselves, do not know how they perceive life. Stop for a while and consider that the obsessive drinker has been centred entirely around alcohol, that his awareness has been numbed by that chemical in his system; as a result of this, his relationships have been thrown out of kilter and his feelings have been anaesthetized. This supports the conclusion that recovery is a process — a maturing process that allows the alcoholic to regain the life that he lost from the time the compulsive drinking started.

Perhaps one of the most frightening issues of becoming well is the acceptance of 'normal' human feelings like fear, anger, resentment, or love and peacefulness. Many people used alcohol to hide away from the discomfort that the painful feelings caused and the sense of vulnerability that came from experiencing the tender ones. Recovery does not make those emotions disappear. In fact, after the alcohol has been out of the system for a short period of time, they have a frightening habit of flooding back with overwhelming intensity and can produce feelings of panic. This is one of the many reasons why it is imperative that the recovering alcoholic sees the need for support from others as a priority. His recovery requires gentle nurturing in its early development.

The decision to give up alcohol can leave a huge, empty void in the life of the recovering alcoholic. Although he has come to recognise that if he wants to live, he has no choice other than to abstain, in doing so he is actually giving up his most important relationship. The alcoholism may have been extremely destructive yet, it was around the liquid in the bottle that he has centred his life. He has put most of his time, energy and thinking into scheming how and when he will have his next drink. Alcohol has been his best friend, the mistress with whom he has had a time-consuming, if ruinous affair. Inevitably, recovery brings a feeling of deprivation and mourning.

Alcohol has been the drinker's god. The challenge of recovery is to find a new god; something to replace the enticing seductiveness of the liquor; something which is positive, rather than destructive; something which gives hope for life, rather than pushing the sufferer closer and closer to death. Something which opens up endless possibilities of unique potential when the alcoholic steps out of his trap and is eventually able to give and receive love. Alcoholics Anonymous provides that for many problem drinkers; the acceptance, the support, the creative thinking, a spiritual programme that attracts recovery and provides a positive centre to one's life.

Replacing Negative Rituals with Positive Ones

Every addictive process involves rituals. The further the alcoholic progresses into his illness, the more ritualised he becomes. These patterns of behaviour are developed to produce some security; some comfort in the predictability. During the addictive process these rituals are often performed alone.

Many alcoholics will get through the week with comparatively little to drink. On Friday evening the drinking ritual starts by leaving work perhaps one hour early; driving round to the supermarket to buy a bottle of spirits, intended to last the weekend, but which never does; dropping into the pub on the pretext of meeting friends, knocking back 3 or 4 large ones, driving home, hiding the bottle in a safe place in the garage; opening a bottle of wine to share with the wife but drinking three-quarters of it himself... Every Friday it's the same pattern over and over again.

Recovery means finding positive rituals to replace the old ones. For the recovering alcoholic who fell into the pattern mentioned above, it might be wise for him to make Friday evening the time for one of his A.A. meetings. Some recovering people like to develop a positive ritual of reading a short passage about recovery each morning and then meditate on what they have just read. This helps form a positive attitude towards getting well for that day.

Finding the Balance

One of the strongest tendencies of an addicted person is to be rather extreme in his behaviour; this can carry on into recovery. It takes time for a recovering person to find the right balance. His obsession for alcohol has been replaced by a more positive hunger for being healthy. He may be aware that he has to restore family relationships, find gainful employment, build up a social life away from alcohol. However, his priority in the early days must be geared towards maintaining his recovery. If he does not have that he may lose everything else. This can be a time of great fear for the alcoholic.

Families who have been really looking forward to the recovery of the addicted drinker may still feel that they are in second place. This time it is the self-help group of A.A. that is taking priority. The closer family relationships are possible, in time. It takes a lot of patience and tolerance on the relative's part as she waits for the alcoholic to become more secure in his recovery.

The Adjustment of the Family to Coping with Recovery

How well the family adjusts to the recovery of the alcoholic depends on how much they have been prepared to look at themselves. If they have recognised a need for changing some of their own attitudes and behaviour and have received help in doing so, then it is likely that they will be able to cope with the adjustment fairly easily. The process is unlikely to be smooth, but it can be dealt with and worked through in time. On the other hand, if a family member is still clinging to the need to be a caretaker, then the recovery of the alcoholic can be an extremely painful time for everyone concerned. Quite often, a codependent person will come face to face with the extent of her addiction during this phase.

Recovery of the alcoholic can bring a great deal of joy to everyone concerned. It is the beginning of a period of hope, when life is taking a turn for the better. There is a tentative belief that the alcoholic is going to have the opportunity to find peace of mind, as well as a more fruitful way of life. It is also a time when those close to the addicted person can relax and be more loving as the tension reduces. The family may find themselves in a period of euphoria. A well-deserved time of joy and gratitude that the alcoholic is recovering. However, in my experience, it never happens that all the benefits of recovery are reaped immediately. Yet, many relatives do expect this.

It would be very unfair and unrealistic of me to lead you to expect that everything is going to be wonderful immediately the alcoholic stops drinking. I have worked with too many people who have been disillusioned by the early stages of recovery. After the years of obsession, pain, stress, anguish and fear, loved ones are often dismayed that recovery does not immediately reach up to their expectations, and that they have to struggle through even more changes. Sadly, in their disappointment, some give up. Life can improve, relationships can become closer, but as well as the alcoholic staying abstinent, recovery often requires some profound adjustments in the family. It demands altering the way that people relate to each other within that group.

I have already written several times that alcoholism is no one's fault and that it is the alcoholic's choice if he drinks alcohol again.

However, I do believe that many well-meaning relatives can undermine the drinker's recovery through their own fear of change. It is one of the saddest experiences in my work to watch an early recovering alcoholic make the painful decision to move away from a family or close friends, because they are helping to make his recovery extremely difficult. Nevertheless, if it is obvious that the caretakers are not willing to change their punishing or controlling attitudes, and if the alcoholic has tried his hardest to cope with the problem, I will support his decision to leave. He may well jeopardise his early fragile recovery if he stays. These relationships may be renewed or restored at a later date when the alcoholic feels stronger in himself. Also, relatives may well benefit from having some space in which to do some introspective thinking, face the reality of their own personal problems and learn how to detach with love.

Conflicting Feelings

Jessie, a friend of mine, described to me her feelings as she watched her husband return home from the treatment centre where he had begun his recovery from alcoholism. He looked well, contented and full of enthusiasm. She felt split down the middle. Part of her was pleased that he had discovered a chance for recovery, that he had found some peace of mind. Another part of her wanted to scream at him that he had no bloody business looking so happy after all the pain and misery his drinking had caused to her and their children. He continued to get well. She continued to become more and more bitter and resentful. Their relationship had changed. She felt he no longer needed her. Jessie refused to get help for herself, not acknowledging that she had a problem. Eventually, they separated and divorced. Despite the fact that they had stayed together through the many years of drinking, trauma and chaos, in recovery the marriage broke down irretrievably. It may not have happened if Jessie had been prepared to admit that she had an overpowering need to caretake, to fix other people's pain. Eventually, she moved into another relationship where she had those needs fed — where she continued to avoid intimacy while she maintained her mothering role.

Many people involved with an alcoholic find that though they have gained what they prayed for (the recovery of the alcoholic), they are also experiencing feelings of loss. It is possible and quite common for relatives to have great relief over the alcoholic's recovery and yet miss the old, terrible, though familiar life-style. Although it was agonizingly painful at times, there were attractions to living with his addiction. For many caretakers, the main positive feelings came from being needed by the alcoholic. He may have been belligerent, abusive or he disappeared for days or weeks at a time. Yet, at the back of the family's mind, it was accepted that he was dependent on them in some way. Recovering alcoholics are more responsible, more independent; this can leave family members, particularly if they are codependent, feeling no longer needed and of little worth. Unless they find other interests in life where they can channel their creativity and build up their self-esteem, recovery of the alcoholic can bring powerful feelings of fear and depression.

During the drinking days the alcoholic is always the centre of attention. That doesn't change much in early recovery. Outsiders to the family who are unaware of what everyone has been through will praise the alcoholic's efforts at recovery. Many family members want to yell, "What about me? Why can't people see that I suffered as much pain as he did?" So many relatives feel left out, frustrated and resentful that the focus appears always to be on him.

The conflict of experiencing gratitude and intense anger can be confusing and frightening. It is very usual, in coping with early recovery, that family members and close friends undergo feelings of extreme bitterness and resentment. This happens especially if they have coped with the drinking days by repressing all their feelings. Often, these surface when people begin to relax, when the alcoholic begins to recover. Insecure relatives who need reassurance of the alcoholic's love may insist that he atone for all the damage done in the past — right away.

As a result, the already low level of trust diminishes even further because the alcoholic can only cope with making amends gradually. Also, relatives may still be putting themselves on a pedestal; that is, judging or trying to fix the alcoholic without looking at how they may have caused harm through their need to control him. Sometimes, because they are feeling uncomfortable, family members can resent the alcoholic because he is starting to feel good. When in pain, it is a very human response to try and make others feel as bad as we do.

Usually, this painful struggle results from a feeling of inadequacy, of uncertainty of not knowing what to expect in the relationship and of no longer knowing how to react.

Changing the Rules

In chapter three, I mentioned the rules that can silently come into being when there is an alcoholic in the family. They were introduced because having these guidelines provided some kind of security. Everyone knew what behaviour to expect from everyone else — including the alcoholic. It was true that he was extremely difficult to live with; probably, he disappeared for days or weeks at a time. However, at some level, the family knew he needed their help; he couldn't function as an active alcoholic without his support system. Within the family, the relationship patterns became rigid and fixed. Everyone knew what role to play — caretaker, tension reliever, scapegoat, peacemaker. Each time he got into trouble with alcohol, the same scene was enacted over and over again with everyone playing their part. Everyone convinced themselves that, "Next time it will be different"; actually very little changed. Perhaps the feelings became more fraught and intense over time.

Recovery of the alcoholic can throw the family into confusion. His getting well means that that group has lost one of its key members; the one person they have all been focusing on. He looks the same, but healthier and more content; as he becomes responsible, he no longer needs looking after; as he is coping with life, there is no more need to worry about him. Quite suddenly, rules and relationships need to change. Everyone is floundering because the old, rigid security has broken down. How are people to react? What does the caretaker do now that she is no longer needed in the same way? What do we talk about now that alcoholism is no longer the topic of the day, or the week, or the month? Why (when this is all I've prayed for) am I so frightened, and feeling lost and inadequate? Where do I fit in?

Many relatives will find themselves reacting to the insecurity by trying to reassert their powerful, caretaking role. This can also arise because of the lack of trust. It takes a long time for that to return completely, if ever. Most recovering alcoholics are aware that that is something they have to try and earn back. In the early stages of recovery, family members can find themselves reluctant to hand over some of the responsibilities to the alcoholic in case he lets them down again. Others have enjoyed being in the position of holding the family reins and don't want to give them up for that reason. More people are frightened to surrender the power because that means allowing themselves to be vulnerable again.

Caretakers who have difficulty in giving up that role will keep themselves in a very powerful position by assuming the right to be the alcoholic's counsellor; checking his behaviour and advising him on how he should think, feel and act. Serious and painful conflict can arise among many couples when one is trying to gain control over the other. Easy relationships only develop when each has learned to let go of the other and allows him to be responsible for himself. Also, each person should be prepared to assess his own progress and make some gradual changes of attitude and behaviour.

Some families can go to the opposite extreme and give the alcoholic too much power within the family circle. Usually, this is as a result of continuing fear and the prolonged belief that anything they say may make the alcoholic drink again. As a result, there is no dialogue and no negotiating of new roles. In such families, individuals pussyfoot around and pander to the recovering alcoholic's expectations: they avoid rocking the boat. There is no chance of mutual trust developing in this kind of relationship, because it continues to be dominated by fear.

Many relationships survive and bloom as a result of the painful struggles of early recovery. Those that have achieved a feeling of togetherness have found this from not having too high expectations too soon; from recognising that recovery from alcoholism and obsessive caretaking provides a new relationship which needs time to develop; from the slow growth of trust; from the gaining of mutual respect and honesty; from the recognition and acceptance that each person needed time and space to heal; from much patience and love.

Part IV

The Freedom to Be

7

Facing Shame

"If we flee from the evil in ourselves, we do it at our hazard. All evil is
potential vitality in need of transformation. To live without the
creative potential of our own destructiveness is to be a cardboard
angel."

If You Meet the Buddha on the Road, Kill Him , Sheldon B. Kopp

It is my belief that recovery from any addiction is twofold. For the
alcoholic, the first part was described in the last chapter "Learning to
Live without Alcohol"; for the caretaker, recovery starts at detaching
with love, as illustrated in chapter five. Staying abstinent, working
through the grief process for the loss of the addiction, learning to
cope with life without the obsession; these all demand a lot of time
and energy. So does experiencing the feelings that previously have
been submerged and are now surfacing. Similarly, the healing of
relationships and making amends for past wrongs are time-
consuming. These are the preoccupations of the initial stages of
recovery.

The second phase starts when many recovering persons become
aware that despite all their hard work, they are still feeling bad. This is
when they are ready to face their shame. This can happen after
months, sometimes years of abstinence from alcohol or refraining
from obsessively caretaking others. Many people who are steeped in
shame don't know it because it disguises itself well.

Shame and addiction come hand in hand. It is unlikely that you

~~ind one without the other. Shame is an inner sense of being ~~ufficient or worthless as a human being. It is a self-judgement ~~which decides that one is fundamentally bad, deeply defective, inadequate and not worthy of love. It is the pain of profound humiliation.

Recovering alcoholics and codependants feel shameful about the way they were during their addictive processes: the shame of being out of control, of behaving in ways that go against the individual's value system. Many caretakers have the belief that their capacity for loving fell short of the mark. Yet, probably, that feeling of worthlessness was there before the addictions took hold. Budding alcoholics drank to make themselves feel better; caretakers obsessively loved others to try and improve their already low self-esteem. Both parties felt bad, isolated, not complete, not good enough, long before the first drinking binge or first obsessive relationship. The pain caused by the brutal self-criticism and self-abuse is so intense that the soul cries out for something to ease that indescribable feeling of emotional paralysis. The alcoholic reached for a drink: the caretaker sought someone else's agony to nurse.

The Difference between Shame and Guilt

It is important that before we develop this theme much further we clarify the difference between shame and guilt. The two often come lumped together and shame can often be dismissed because the guilt has been faced and dealt with. However, although they are both a feeling of 'badness', they are quite different.

Guilt is the easiest to identify, understand and do something about. It results from doing something we know is wrong; like lying, stealing or belittling a loved one. Guilt happens when we break our own rules. Guilt reveals itself in self-reproaches like, "How could I have *done* that?" The resolution for guilt comes through making amends, atoning for what we have done.

Shame is more insidious than guilt. The shameful person will reproach **himself**, not what he has done. "What an idiot *I* am!", is an exclamation of self-judgement, of shame. A human who is full of shame has a tendency to be all or nothing: "If I can't love everyone, then I can't love anyone", is a typical attitude of such a person. Shame is not easily resolved. Facing shame means facing the extremes in ourselves, facing the evil and the good, the beast and the angel, and discovering that we are actually somewhere in the middle, a mixture of both: that means accepting our humanness, our ordinariness, our limitations.

Addiction to Perfection

Over generations our society has become more and more preoccupied with favouring people who have goals to achieve and aim to be successful in life. What we produce, how intellectually bright we are, how good we appear — these are what are valued. Few people are told that they are alright just the way they are. The message absorbed by many of us as we grow up and don't achieve the goals that are set by parents and others in authority, is that we are not good enough. Much shame is rooted in many family rules and myths inherited over generations. We believe that in order to be loved, we have to attain those targets. That drive can become compulsive. As we get older, we are rarely satisfied by our progress. If we don't attain these goals, it endorses that feeling of being inadequate. If we do reach them, then for some reason, those of us who are shame-based are not satisfied and set out to prove to ourselves and others that we can achieve even more. Our goal becomes perfection. In seeking that perfection, we deny parts of ourselves and exaggerate others; we become obsessively driven, trying to reach that impossible god-like state. In so doing, we become isolated, cut off from the mainstream of life; frozen into acting out a role and denying the reality of ourselves.

People who reach for perfection have a secret side to themselves. A side that they have learned to hide, because to allow others to see it brings the fear of rejection or abandonment. They have difficulty in trusting others and are terrified of intimacy or being vulnerable in case that secret side is found out. Sadly, because so much effort is going into denying the beast in them they are living the life of 'cardboard angels'. A shameful person is longing for love — yet terrified of it, and is trying to find acceptance through being something other than they are. So many alcoholics, so many caretakers are denying themselves the richness of their lives because they are square pegs who are painfully trying to force themselves into round holes.

How Shame Can Disguise Itself

Shame has many masks. It hides in the dark and lies dormant, protecting itself from being brought out into the light. To experience shame is to experience exposure; uncovering unacknowledged and unrecognised parts of the personality. The pain of uncovering shame is in exposing those intimate, vulnerable aspects of the self to one's self. To let others see our shame is often embarrassing and painful, but the greatest agony is in facing our own imperfection.

There are two kinds of intense fear in shame. First, is the fear of punishment, the belief that if I am found out I will be penalised. The second fear is of abandonment, of rejection, of being left alone if the other person knew how bad I was.

Shame can be incommunicable. It hides behind rage, depression, controlling, inflexibility, numbed feelings, grandiosity, intolerance, blaming others, and extreme anxiety: all feelings or behaviours which stop others from getting close and keep us isolated. Denial is an integral part of shame — the denial of who one is. One of the ways we avoid feeling our shame is to stay rigid and try and remain in control of our lives and those around us. Trying to stay one step ahead, ready to deal with anything that might pop up unexpectedly, aiming for set goals, anticipating the problems and frightened of change. Controlling in this manner means we are living to set rules and regulations, not allowing for flexibility or spontaneity. People who are perfectionists tend to have high expectations of everyone, including themselves, and are often angry and judgemental when those expectations are not lived up to.

The more shameful we are, the more we strive for control; the more we need release from that rigid lifestyle, the more our starving, repressed energy channels itself into compulsive behaviours; the more shameful we are . . . It is a roundabout of pain and more pain that can go on and on; that is, until we have the courage to face our shame and step away from the vicious circling, unencumbered by the restrictions of perfectionism.

The Dry Drunk and Other Addictions

Many alcoholics can stop drinking but unless they achieve some inner peace, staying sober can be miserable for themselves and those close to them. To stop drinking and not face shame requires coping with life with clenched fists and white knuckles. Unless the dry alcoholic faces his shame, accepts himself as he is (a mixture of both beast and angel) then he is going to keep his defences up. He is going to stay angry, controlling, inflexible, grandiose, intolerant, almost paranoid and extremely anxious. Many relatives who have lived with a 'dry drunk' have often found themselves wishing that he would start drinking again because that seemed easier to handle.

Yet, this condition does not just apply to alcoholics. Compulsive caretakers and other addicted people can find themselves as defensive when they abstain from their primary addiction. They, too, can be difficult to live with if they have not given up their ideals of perfectionism and surrendered to the process of life.

It is not unusual for someone who has been involved in one addiction to progress onto other compulsive behaviours. Some people can be cross-addicted; that is, addicted to more than one substance or activity at one time. People can find themselves addicted to alcohol and tranquillizers simultaneously; or alcohol and gambling; or caretaking and overeating; or caretaking and compulsive house-cleaning; or alcohol and caretaking. Others can find themselves moving from one compulsion to another. Maria's history illustrates this well.

Maria was a well-known model. When she was at the height of her profession she was obsessed with staying thin; the more preoccupied she became about her figure, the more out of control her eating became. As she panicked about putting on weight, she would binge on food and them make herself sick. Maria's first addiction was bulimia. However, she found tranquillizers when her doctor prescribed them for her anxiety, and for a while her eating problem abated. Maria started to obsess about her tranquillizers as much as she had about food. For years she took more than prescribed and after an overdose, decided that she needed to come off drugs. Then the withdrawals were so uncomfortable that she had a glass of sherry to help her feel better and ended up drinking the whole bottle. Although she had drunk socially before, that was the beginning of her alcoholism. Ten agonizing years later she ended up unemployed and in a treatment centre for alcoholism where she was helped to come off both tranquillizers and alcohol. For a while, she was reasonably happy and then her eating problem began again. She was eating compulsively and gaining a lot of weight.

Compulsive behaviour does not necessarily vanish because the primary addiction has been treated. Many recovering alcoholics will find themselves compulsively smoking, eating, wheeling and dealing, gambling, hoarding, shopping, working or involved in compulsive sexual behaviours or compulsive caretaking. Whilst these addictions may not have the same urgent threat of death as alcoholism — the obsession, the secrecy, the dishonesty, the compulsive drive, the need for the feeling of release, form the same pattern as the primary illness and could lead right back to it. Alternatively, the addicted person could stay in his second addiction living a double life, swinging between perfectionism and loss of control, still isolated and cut off from others. This can also have painful repercussions on loved ones. Whether he is enabled in doing that depends on the health of his family and where they are in their recovery from caretaking and shame.

Addictive behaviours continue because there is a huge reservoir of shame which has not been confronted. Also, because of this there is an overwhelming need to be defensive, rigid and in control. It seems that the more we deny our limitations, the more powerless and out of control we become.

Addicted caretakers can also have problems with other compulsions like eating, drinking, workaholism, cleanliness, shoplifting, gambling etc. Alternatively, they can keep changing their relationships so that they have subsequent subjects for their obsessive caretaking.

Shoulds and Shouldn'ts

People who are full of shame, who are perfectionists and rigid in thought and behaviour, use the words 'should' and 'shouldn't' often. Frequently, statements like the following are thought or uttered. "He *shouldn't* have drank so much at the office party. He *should* have known better." Or, "I *should* have been able to stop him", "They *should* have understood that he was under a lot of stress".

Should is a word that restricts, controls, condemns and gives no freedom of choice. It limits our relationships because others shy away from our intolerance and need to control. The use of such language helps form restricting rules which do not allow the development of the creativity of the individual. Time and time again, in our drive for perfection, we destroy our spontaneity, our uniqueness, our acceptance of ourselves. We place very high expectations on our own abilities. We demand that we *should* know better or *should* do better than we have already done. We increase our shame, our low self-esteem because we see ourselves as having fallen short of the mark.

Healing from shame starts when we learn to be more gentle with ourselves, to value who we are. In order to do that, we need to moderate our use of the word 'should'. We need to give ourselves choices, allow ourselves to be imperfect, give ourselves permission to make mistakes. Above all, we need to forgive ourselves for being human beings — not God. To heal from the ravages of shame, we need to learn to love ourselves.

Recovering from Shame

Recovering from shame requires finding the courage to be: the courage to accept that we are human beings. Therefore, we understand that we are limited in our humanity and not perfect: as human beings we are vulnerable and we need help. Addicts deny their need for assistance from other people; the alcoholic believes he gets the help he needs from the bottle; the caretaker is convinced that she is there to meet the need of others. Recovering from shame starts when we reach out to others and seek help; when we gradually let our defences down and show our vulnerability.

In order to heal from the devastating effects of shame we need to risk exposure and that means we have to choose very carefully who we are vulnerable with. It is important that the person you choose is someone who has faced his or her own shame, is non-judgemental, is accepting of who you are, is centred in themselves and doesn't have rigid rules and requirements of the way you should or shouldn't be. Above all, seek someone you trust, someone with whom you can build a relationship. I believe that it is also important that that person is the same sex as yourself. When dealing with sensitive matters around shame it is easy to get distracted by issues that come up in a close relationship with a member of the opposite sex. Perhaps a sponsor in

Al-Anon or Alcoholics Anonymous will fill the requirement: someone who has been working on their recovery for some years. Alternatively, a therapist or counsellor who understands addiction and its relationship with shame will supply the much-needed support.

The relationship between the sponsor or therapist and sufferer of shame is all-important because therapy for shame is love: not romantic love but spiritual love. The acceptance of one's humanity, one's imperfections, one's limitations as well as one's gifts and talents. It requires a meeting of equals, a two-way reciprocal relationship where the helper is objective and yet caring. The traditional psychiatrist/patient where the psychiatrist is a giver but not a receiver does not help heal shame. Indeed, it can increase the feeling of worthlessness. The healing of shame comes through sharing vulnerability. Security comes from knowing that the sponsors or therapists are not striving for perfection but are accepting their humanness, their limitations and are believing that they are good enough, the way they are.

Healing from shame takes time: it is a spiritual journey. It requires telling our story; it demands really feeling the depth of our shame. It means coming to accept that our lives cannot be controlled by willpower but that we have to surrender and trust life. When we confront shame we become aware of a void, a spiritual hunger. However, as we risk and expose our vulnerabilities and are accepted we come to see that we need not be god-like, but human, a mixture of beast and angel, and in that acceptance of our limitations we find a feeling of wholeness. In forgiving ourselves for being human, we find we no longer have that sense of isolation: we have a feeling of belonging, of oneness with the universe and all around us.

The positive side of addiction and shame is that the pain pushes us to be who we are meant to be and frees us to truly love and be loved. The healing of shame is paraphrased in the following quotation —

> 'I need' because 'I hurt' — if deepest need is honest. What I need is another's hurt, another's need. Such a need on my part would be 'sick' — if the other had not the same need of me, of my hurt and my need. Because we share hurt, we can share healing. Because we know need, we can heal each other.
>
> Our mutual healing will not be the healing of curing but the

healing of caring. To heal is to make whole. Curing makes whole from the outside: it is good healing, but it cannot touch my deepest need, my deepest hurt — my shame, the dread of myself that I harbour within. Caring makes whole from within: it reconciles me to myself — as-I-am.

But I can care, can become whole, only if you care enough — need enough — to share your shame with me.

Could the same be true for you?

Shame and Guilt; Characteristics of the Dependency Cycle, Ernest Kurtz

For me, those words describe the healing that takes place in self-help groups like Alcoholics Anonymous, Al-Anon, Adult Children of Alcoholics and Alateen. There, many people can find the beginning of the acknowledgement that — I am who I am. I am accepted and loved just as I am; and I accept and love myself and others just as we are. Something that has been missing from their lives for a long time.

8

Relationships and Recovery

"By consistently choosing Love rather than fear, we can experience a personal transformation which enables us to be more naturally loving to ourselves and others. In this way we can begin to recognise and experience the Love and joy that unites us."

Love is Letting Go of Fear, Gerald G. Jampolsky

If it is allowed to, fear can paralyse many recovering alcoholics and caretakers. Most human beings are seeking a loving relationship with at least one other person. Addiction to alcohol or alcoholics has hindered the search for intimacy. It is impossible to have a close, honest, equal relationship with another human being if the most important love affair is with an intoxicating liquid in a bottle. That tantalizing chemical distorts reality, numbs feelings, destroys value systems and demands a lot of the alcoholic's time and energy. Although in the early stages of the illness it lowered inhibitions and gave the drinker courage to be more vulnerable, its seductive promise of intimacy was a lie. In fact, alcoholism destroys relationships, pushing the sufferer into a pit of isolation.

Equally, the obsessive caretaker has also avoided close intimate relationships. Few codependent people find it easy to be vulnerable, hiding behind a façade of being a coper. Many are aching to be accepted for who they really are, but cannot find the key that will assist them in letting down that front. The obsession with the alcoholic takes up a lot of the caretaker's time and she is too exhausted and defensive to find the energy to reach out to others and let them move in more closely.

Recovery from any addiction means a healing of the self. Loving relationships are an important factor in restoring that person back to emotional, spiritual and physical health. To be able to survive in this life, people need to believe that they are worthwhile to themselves and others. In order to love and be loved, we have to be convinced of our worth as human beings: we have to love ourselves. I also believe that we have to feel complete in ourselves, at peace with ourselves: whole persons. If not, we search for relationships which will fill our psychological and emotional holes. That is, an individual will transfer upon his or her partner all of the unmet needs that he or she failed to get at some important developmental point in life. Tragically, if this happens, partners find themselves locked into an impossible relationship which often ends in bitterness toward the person who is unable to complete the other. Often in such a relationship there is a terror of abandonment by one partner, and a fear of engulfment by the other. The more one clings, the more the other wants to run.

Many people find that they have problems with intimacy in early recovery. Often this is shown through sexual problems. Examples of these might be:-

— the couple where the alcoholic has been sober for two years and, during that time, they have not made love once;

— the young man who is desperately seeking a close relationship but has never been able to 'chat up' a woman sober and is terrified of doing so;

— the young woman who believes that all she has got to offer the men in her life is the quality of her sexual performance and is compulsively jumping in and out of different beds. She is in a terrible conflict because of her feelings of guilt and shame about her promiscuity;

— the middle aged woman who is still processing her guilt, fear, anger and anxiety which she first surfaced in a treatment programme for alcoholism. She had suppressed all those feelings for 25 years when she had an incestuous relationship with her alcoholic father.

A large number of alcoholics have learned to become sexual beings only with the help of alcohol or drugs. Initially, many are afraid of making love sober. For some that fear is akin to panic. Many codependants are surprised that they no longer enjoy sex when they lose that caretaking role. Somehow, the loss of that defence brings a frightening vulnerability. Others have suffered so much emotional pain in the relationship during the drinking days. To surrender to the close intimacy of a loving, sexual relationship requires a lot of trust and that is rarely present in the early days of recovery.

Seeking Intimacy in Recovery

Frequently, the trap in our loving relationship is that we seek complete intimacy with one 'special' person. Often, many assume that close relationships begin in bed. Many recovering addicts are disappointed because, in their eagerness to find an intimate relationship, they find that by being sexually active with another, they have found a greater intimacy, but, it is not enough. They have put the emphasis on being friendly lovers rather than loving friends.

Many have to discover that real closeness comes from friendship, from building up trust, from exposing our vulnerability, from sharing a variety of experiences with another. Also, some people have to find that there are several different kinds of close, familiar relationships; that an intimate experience does not automatically build an intimate relationship. Equally important is the recognition that intimacy is a process which grows with time. It is never completed nor fully accomplished.

Frequently, both the alcoholic and the caretaker have unrealistically high expectations of the kind of relationship that the process of healing brings. This is because they have previously avoided or missed out on human closeness as a result of the preoccupation with alcohol or the addicted drinker. As a result, they hungrily reach for the dream which previously has eluded them.

Recovery and peace of mind do attract closer relationships on all sorts of levels with a variety of people. The isolation is gradually broken as the recovering person finds friendship with others by sharing some of the following kinds of communication:-

Intellectual Closeness which comes from sharing ideas, opinions, beliefs, theories or philosophies with another. This kind of relationship helps us think out loud, clarifying and developing our ideas.

Occupational Closeness which comes from sharing a job or career with someone else, while building up trust and the ability to work as part of a team.

Social Closeness which comes from friendship groups or community groups. Many recovering alcoholics and caretakers find this kind of relationship in Alcoholics Anonymous, Al-Anon, Adult Children of Alcoholics Groups and Alateen. Alternatively, church groups or youth groups also help us share in group activities.

Recreational Closeness which comes from sharing hobbies, sports, fun or other interests outside work. The 'team spirit' which comes from sharing in activities like football, rugby, cricket, etc, often provides a special kind of bonding.

Aesthetic Closeness which comes from sharing the beauty of the world with another — whether in enjoying the pleasures of art, music, literature or the qualities of our environment. The close communication that can come from sharing these kinds of experience does not always have to be spoken about.

Affectionate Closeness which comes from family and close friends through touch and other experiences of affection. This can come through hugging, exchanging fond looks, tender smiles, or holding hands perhaps.

Sexual Closeness which comes from enjoying an intimate, physical relationship with another, usually culminating in sexual intercourse. The strength of the bond in this kind of relationship depends on how committed and loving the friendship is.

Emotional Closeness which comes from sharing one's deep feelings and vulnerabilities in a mutually trusting relationship; from expressing warmth, tenderness and love. Also, this kind of relationship can provide a 'safe place' to share some 'difficult' feelings such as anger or loneliness.

Spiritual Closeness can result from the peak experience of sharing a similar belief of meaning in life. One kind of spiritual intimacy results in a feeling of 'oneness' with another human being and yet being aware of and comfortable with one's separateness. It is not synonymous with religion although it can be experienced in that context. Another kind of spiritual closeness is a feeling of peace and security which comes from accepting the presence of a Higher Power or an awareness of Love in one's life.

Many recovering people discover that an intimate relationship is one in which persons feel closeness in several of the types mentioned above. This is usually accompanied by the expectation that the relationship and the experiences will continue over time. However, intimacy can be blocked by wanting too much, too soon.

Some Unreal Expectations which Lead to Disappointment in Early Recovery

I have mentioned that alcoholics and their partners often have unrealistically high hopes of what recovery will bring to their marriage. These are some of the more common assumptions of people who have been involved in aftercare programmes of treatment centres and who have found problems in their relationships.

Most people in long-term partnerships expect that recovery from alcoholism means immediate improvement in sexual relationships

Actually, I have met very few recovering couples where this is the case. A good sexual relationship requires a lot of trust. For most, early recovery means working through considerable fear, anger, feelings of shame, low self-esteem and suspiciousness. Many women (alcoholic and non-alcoholic) may find themselves anorgasmic (unable to have orgasm) due to sexual fears, perhaps as a result of forced intercourse during the drinking days. Another reason may be the fear of letting go. The assumption is that if they give power to their partner, they may lose control, become too vulnerable and get hurt again. Repressed anger prevents a number of women from fully enjoying sex. Many alcoholic women and partners of alcoholic men find a number of submerged resentments surfacing in early recovery. These block any kind of intimacy until the feelings can be resolved.

Some men may find that they have to cope with continued impotence for a time. This results from having had too much alcohol in the system. A period of not being able to perform sexually can threaten the sense of their masculinity and result in feelings of failure and anxiety. Sometimes, unless these men get help in dealing with their feelings of inadequacy, this can lead to resumed drinking. Often, the caretaking partner may also suffer from a period of worry and fear at this time. She, too, needs support in accepting that the impotence is not her fault; that she is not the cause, that she is not sexually inferior. If the problems persist, then the couple may need help from a marital or sexual counsellor.

Rigid attitudes towards male or female roles

This is slowly changing, but for many, the stereotype of a man is still to be strong, aggressive, liking sports and being the chief breadwinner in the family. A woman is expected to be soft, pretty, passive, to like babies and be the chief homemaker.

Usually, the man is expected to take the lead and be the expert in sexual relating. Many men — not only alcoholic men — have felt very threatened by the more sexually assertive women produced in the last few decades. Yet, a number of women have sat in my office bemoaning the fact that they haven't enjoyed their lover's lovemaking. When questioned if they have discussed this fact with their partners, there is usually an embarrassed silence followed by a comment like, "No, because I feel it would threaten his masculinity. He would be hurt", or, "No, because he is the man and he is supposed to know".

Communication is a big problem for many couples in early recovery, and perhaps for a number of people the most difficult area to discuss is what they like and need sexually.

In recovery, many men continue to isolate themselves from others by denying their tender feelings. They may have had several 'successful' affairs performance-wise or be living with or married to another person. However, they continue to be exceedingly lonely because they do not know how to be vulnerable and form close, intimate relationships. This does not apply only to alcoholic men. It is a well-known fact that, these days one in three marriages end in marital breakdown. In seven out of ten of those marriages, the divorce is sued for by the woman in the relationship. The reason often given is that the men have either never learned, or have forgotten the language of their feelings and it is costing them their relationships. Sadly, in many circles, it is still seen to be unmanly to cry or to show any strong emotion other than aggression. Many men have been brought up to avoid intimacy or vulnerability. "Big boys don't cry". Too often, being male means handling one's problems all alone. Sadly, many suffer from intense feelings of isolation because of this.

The romantic myth that two people who pair will become 'as one'

Perhaps this is the myth that causes most damage in many relationships. Society leads us to believe that this is the ideal way to be with someone we love. For people who have previously experienced the partnership as a living hell during the drinking days, this dream provides much false hope and temporary relief. However, this kind of marriage, where the feeling of well-being of one partner is entirely dependent on the approval of the other, can end up stifling and destroying the warmth and love between the couple. In the drive to end the sense of isolation and being irrelevant, people often find themselves trapped in a web of neediness. This placing such high expectations on the other partner stops each individual from taking responsibility for his or her individual growth.

So often, we come across relationships where both partners are struggling for recovery. Frequently, the healing of that partnership has reached a stalemate position because one person is looking at the other, pointing the finger accusingly and saying that the way he or she is, is not enough. Statements are made like, "Our marriage would be perfect, if only *you* would change some of your attitudes and behaviour". The power struggle which was evident during the drinking days can still continue in sobriety. Possibly, this tug-of-war will persist until the relationship founders as a result of this destructive attitude. Alternatively, one or both partners may receive the message that the only way the partnership will survive is if they respect the other enough to 'let go' or 'detach with love' — thus allowing the other partner to be responsible for his or her own individual growth. Eventually, it has to be understood that the only person I have the power to change is myself.

Only beautiful people are sexually attractive

Perfectionism and low self-esteem are the greatest inhibitors of any loving relationship. Our culture has taught us through advertising and the media, that only certain faces and bodies are beautiful and that sexual attractiveness is reserved for people who possess those assets. Many young people (and not so young people) in early recovery are convinced that various parts of their anatomies are too small, too large, too ugly and therefore no one is going to be attracted to them. Those of more mature years grieve for their youthful bodies and some fear that they have 'passed it'.

Fear of rejection often attracts that very reaction. Some people who have problems in asserting themselves may find that when they take risks and approach a member of the opposite sex, indeed, they are turned down. The negative thinking is reinforced. Automatically, the conviction is, "There is something the matter with me. I *am* sexually unattractive". People locked into this kind of attitude probably need to take time to face their shame and feelings of sexual inadequacy. They may need some help in improving their self-esteem.

Only heterosexual relationships are normal

A very high proportion of the gay/lesbian population is alcoholic. Some studies suggest that two to three of every four homosexuals are chemically dependent. Acceptance of who one is, is one of the most important factors of recovery. Being loved and accepted by others is also of great value in the healing process of addiction. The homosexual person is often in a double-bind. To accept his or her sexual idenfication is to differentiate in an unacceptable way to much of the population, perhaps even to his family. To reject the homosexuality is to deny that person's identity. So many gay people revert to drinking as a result of feeling 'not normal'.

Some people need time in recovery to discover what their sexual preferences are. Sometimes during the drinking days, people become involved in same-sex relationships. Only after a period of staying sober can they actually tell if they are heterosexual, bisexual or homosexual.

Finding Healthy Relationships

Many people find that warm intimate relationships come from lowering expectations and not anticipating too much too soon. Pushing towards unrealistic dreams produces feelings of frustration, disappointment, anger, impatience and intolerance. Loving partnerships live in the now, accepting and valuing the present time.

A central factor in gaining satisfying relationships is the respect of one partner for the other. This comes as each individual becomes more centred in the loving part of themselves as opposed to the side that is dominated by fear. In that state of peacefulness, of self-acceptance, it is easier to have reverence for the other. Careful listening and valuing what the other person says shows respect. Having a sense of self (as described in chapter five) is also another way of being respectful. Responding out of my own honesty and vulnerability shows that I value you, I value myself, I value our relationship. So often, in the past, I have devalued both of us and the love between us because I have been fearful, judgemental and wanting to control. I have loved when I was getting what I thought I wanted and hated when I didn't get what I thought I wanted.

Intimacy becomes a predictable by-product of owning a sense of self. Anger, fear, hurt, and loneliness are expressed differently by someone who is valuing their uniqueness. Relatives can hear the quality of self-expression as it is shared in an assertive, non-threatening, non-blaming way. They feel respected and not judged or put-down.

In order to find love, it is important to have peace of mind. This means reducing the obsessions, the rushing around. It means making peace of mind our priority. So often, in our crazy drive to find peace of mind through perfection, we increase our fear by trying to achieve as much as we can. Perhaps in our efforts to find security, we try to gather as many material possessions as we can, we try to live as long a life as we can. At the same time, we try to advance our careers, travel and see as much of the world as we can, be as loving as we can, be as sexually exciting as we can and gain as much approval from others as we can. So much energy is going into trying to achieve, that we avoid what we are desperately seeking. Intimacy eludes us because we can't stand still long enough to receive it.

Paradoxically, many find in recovery that intimacy grows

through detachment. They learn that in a caring relationship detaching lovingly means learning to live side by side, not in each other's pockets. The goal in such a partnership is not dependence on another, but healthy belonging. A fulfilling, mature, loving togetherness gives each individual the right to find the freedom to be.

Indeed, healthy intimate relationships only become possible when one finds a wholeness, a feeling of completeness and does not need to be dependent on another. Spiritual teachers tell us that the first stage of spiritual growth is learning to love and accept oneself; that means taking time to come to terms with who one is. Only when we begin to be comfortable with ourselves can we reach out and genuinely give unconditional love to others; only then can we believe that we deserve what others are offering us; only then can we begin to develop intimate relationships.

To summarise; we can develop healthy relationships by:

Encouraging the individuality and uniqueness of the other

The growth of both partners is the ideal of a mature relationship, even if they are progressing in different ways. Such freedom is possible because of the respect and trust in the relationship. Conflict is not seen as a threat, but is accepted as part of everyday life. Because the couple are relaxed and value each other's point of view, they are usually able to resolve the conflict through discussion. They know that the closeness allows for personal differences. The partnership is flexible enough to cope with major changes in an individual. Perhaps that person has learned to let 'the self' emerge instead of acting out a role or pattern that has been established since childhood. Also, people are allowed to take risks and make mistakes in such a relationship because personal limitations are also accepted. It is much easier to solve problems within those limits.

Sharing feelings spontaneously

People within a healthy relationship value their self-esteem. The level of trust being high gives permission to each to be free to be themselves without fear of rejection. Feelings can be expressed spontaneously instead of being suppressed until a later time, when they explode in a destructive tirade, or implode causing much physical and mental pain. Being intimates means sharing vulnerabilities, dreams, hopes, fears. Also, such a close relationship provides the safety for choosing to tell secrets. We are all entitled to privacy, but secrets about matters that make us feel shameful cut us off from intimacy. Blocks in communication are removed and closeness deepens when we choose to tell a loved one of our hidden shame.

Putting the same value on receiving and giving

Being intimate means we accept that we are accepted. It also means that one can give without expecting to receive in return. In dependent relationships, many people cannot believe that they are accepted for who they are. Instead, they trade conditional love; the attitude being, I am proving to you that I love you — now, in return I expect you to love me in the way I want. Healthy relationships free both partners from dancing the steps of that old familiar destructive dance. Both receiving and giving can be done without obligation.

Understanding that each person needs time and space on their own, away from the relationship

This is not the kind of need as in a dependent relationship where one partner has to be cut off from the other to protect himself, or needs to feel free to breathe, away from the stifling closeness. Instead, it is a profound trust that allows one to be away from the other, knowing that he or she will return, that the love continues in the absence of that person.

Valuing commitment

Commitment can be seen by many as a 'loss of self'; as an experience of being taken over. It can be quite terrifying for some. However, in a healthy relationship commitment is experienced as a genuine concern for the well-being of the other person. It is an act of love. It accepts without resistance the importance and value of the other person in one's life.

Affirming the equality of self and partner

In healthy loving, both people enjoy the power that comes from self-confidence, self-love and a mutual love for each other. Both partners recognise and accept each other as equals. They are not caught up in power struggles where one tries to out-manipulate the other. Individual and mutual respect keeps the relationship on a par, where each is free to be.

Recovery from addiction is an adventure. It can be very exciting. It is possible to stagnate, to remain free from alcohol or reduce the obsession for the alcoholic; to live like this and yet not grow. Intimacy is a closeness, a warm, intense, caring and involved relationship. People who are alcoholic or who have lived with alcoholism need and deserve it as much as anyone else. The answer is discovered by pushing the fears aside and finding the courage to be who one is truly meant to be — an important, but unique human being who can both give and receive love.

Part V

Children in an Alcoholic Family — The Next Link in the Chain

9

The Hidden Victims

"At nights, I sit on the stairs, listening to them fighting. I can't sleep. I worry about what is going to happen next."

Sophie, *aged nine, daughter of an alcoholic*

I met Sophie six years ago. Her father, Ian, had been in treatment for a month. His wife and two elder children, both in their late teens, had been visiting him regularly, but I noticed Sophie had not come to see her father. When I asked why, I was told that their youngest daughter was too young to understand what was going on, that she had been protected from the knowledge of father's alcoholism. The family felt that to bring her to see him in a treatment centre would only upset her. They wanted to shield her from what was happening.

Two or three days after that discussion with the family, Ian came to see me. He had been talking to another patient whose children of a similar age had been discussing their mother's drinking behaviour with her. He had been shocked at the level of their awareness and wondered if Sophie was as unaware as he had first assumed. The outcome of our conversation was that he asked me to meet with his daughter.

Sophie was a bright young girl and after a cautious start to our meeting, once she realised that she had her parents' permission to talk about the drinking, the floodgates opened. She talked and talked and talked. One of her problems had been that she was extremely aware of what was going on, but she realised that everyone in the family became very uncomfortable when the subject of her father's drinking came up. They even asked her to leave the room on several occasions. Her family was unaware that she sat on the stairs and listened. She had learned the 'no-talking rule' quickly and early in her life.

Sophie had not put the label 'alcoholism' on her father's condition, but she knew something was wrong, knew her father behaved differently from other fathers, knew her family was not as warm, open and loving as those of some of her friends. She sensed an insecure, uncomfortable atmosphere in the house. Sophie reeled off a list of behaviours and situations that she had never talked about before.

She knew her father smelled 'funny' a lot of the time, that he couldn't talk properly, that he fell over, that his hands shook. She knew he was ill, but she didn't know what the illness was.

She knew that her father hid bottles in the house and in the garden. She knew that he drank too much. Someone at school had told her that her father was a drunk.

Sometimes, when she was in the car with him, she was frightened because he didn't seem to be in control.

On one occasion, she met him coming in the front door with blood running down his face. Her mother sent her to her room and wouldn't tell her what had happened.

Sophie knew her mother was very angry at her father. She kept talking about leaving him but never did it. Sometimes their arguments at night were very violent with dishes and furniture being thrown. She knew her elder brother would try and protect their mother, often getting hurt himself. This is what Sophie listened to when she sat on the stairs; not one isolated incident of violence, but several.

She knew her mother kept moving back into the spare bedroom and then a few nights later back into her parents' bedroom. She heard the arguing late at night.

Sometimes her father wouldn't come home at night and she would hear her mother cry herself to sleep.

She had been told not to bring her schoolfriends home, and a lot of the time she didn't want to. She didn't want her friends to know how much her parents argued.

Sophie felt very protective towards her father. She wished her mother wouldn't nag him so much or shout at him so much. She felt her father needed looking after because, "He didn't know how to look after himself". She said that she had made up her mind that if Mummy left she would stay with Daddy, to see that he got to work, wore clean clothes and ate his meals. A caretaker in the making!

Young Sophie's attitude was very matter-of-fact. This was 'normal' life for her. Her father had been a chronic alcoholic all of her life; her mother had been obsessively preoccupied with him during those years. Sophie was very independent because she had had to be. She was also very isolated. In her own family, she had learned not to ask questions and accepted that the mysteries going on around her were not going to be explained. She lived a lot of her time in her bedroom and in a fantasy world.

Children of Alcoholics are Abused

Sophie's is a very typical story of a child of an addicted drinker. Yet, so often I am assured by the adults that they have been unaffected. The stark reality is that children from a family where there is an alcoholic and an obsessively caretaking parent are abused. At best, they are isolated within the family and their needs are seen as secondary, their feelings are put on ice. At worst, because there are no fixed or defined boundaries of what is appropriate behaviour on the part of the adults in the family, they are witness to physical abuse, sexual abuse and may well be victims of those violations themselves. Alcoholic drinking lowers inhibitions, distorts value systems, changes the personality of the drinker. Children are often on the receiving end of this and are maltreated. Not every alcoholic is violent or a sexual abuser of his children — but, as the disease develops and the drinker moves further away from reality, it can increase the risk that this type of behaviour may happen.

Sometimes, the sexual abuse to the child is not within the family. The alcoholic's preoccupation with alcohol, the caretaker's obsession with the addicted drinker means the children are disregarded. Frequently, they are left to their own devices, wandering the streets late at night, often on their own. Sometimes the abuse is not discovered by concerned persons until years later, if ever. Many children in such families feel they cannot talk to their parents about their problems, seeing them as having enough to cope with.

The codependent person can physically maltreat her children too. Trapped in her desperation and frustration at the alcoholic, she can choose to release some or all of that violent aggression on the youngsters in the family. Often, it is one child who is picked on, the one who doesn't conform, the one who acts out his own feelings of rage, the one who is scapegoated.

The outside world often fails to notice the violence in these families. It is covered up, minimized and kept a secret. The denial of an alcoholic family is so intact, that if anyone has suspicions of maltreatment, the barrier of cohesive protectiveness of that group is difficult to penetrate.

Never Knowing What to Expect Next

Children of alcoholics grow up in an environment where the undercurrent of fear, tension and anxiety is ever present. There is little stable security in the family. Returning home from school, walking in the door is itself a stressful situation because children of addicted drinkers never know what to expect next. Is Mum going to be drunk again? Is she going to yell and scream and shout like she did last night? Is she going to be unconscious like she was last week? What can I do so that I don't upset her? Will Dad stay away again tonight? We hardly ever see him now. The following are some vignettes which illustrate some of the pain of children of alcoholics.

I first became aware of some of the effects of alcoholism on the family when I was a student teacher. I was working with a class of seven year olds. Kelly was one of them; she was a hard worker, very quiet and didn't seem to make friends easily. She didn't have the bubbly spontaneity of many of her other classmates; she was wary and watchful. We were aware of this, but didn't understand why until her mother came to pick her up from school one day, as she quite often did. However, this time it was different. This time Kelly's mum was obviously drunk. She staggered, shouted loudly, slurred her speech and reeked of whisky; she tripped and fell over, swearing as she did it. The children giggled. Kelly cringed, blushed and went to help her mother out of the classroom; she was obviously ashamed and embarrassed.

David and John are brothers aged ten and eleven. John, the elder boy, talks and acts like a fifty-year-old who has all the responsibilities of the world on his shoulders. He is devoted to looking after David. When I was talking to them both John was arranging to take his brother out fishing for the day. He was very concerned because the younger boy was upset. Their alcoholic father had let them down again; he had promised to take them fishing, but had disappeared on yet another drinking binge. Not once did John mention his own distressed feelings to me; his main concern was that David shouldn't be upset. He was trying to provide some stability by being very responsible himself.

Keith and Lisa are twelve and nine. Their 'real' father is alcoholic and so is their step-father. I met them the day they had left their home at two o'clock in the morning, because their step-father had returned to the family drunk and had violently attacked their mother. They were going to live with their 'real' dad. Brother and sister were having an argument about which Dad was the worse alcoholic. Apparently, leaving the house in the middle of the night was a pattern they knew well. Keith said to me in a confidential and prosaic way, "The trouble with Mum is that she is not very good at choosing men. We are always having to get her out of trouble."

Katy is fourteen years old. She is the eldest of three children. Her Mum is a chronic alcoholic. Her Dad, who is the manager of an engineering firm, copes with her mother's alcoholism by working very late and having the occasional affair. Sometimes he is there to support Katy in her role as substitute mother. More often, he stays away and leaves her to struggle. When he doesn't come home, Mum retaliates by drinking more.

Katy is very organised, very practical and very matter-of-fact. Not only has she organised the home, her younger brother and sister, and nursed her mother, but she is a super-achiever at school. Her teachers, who are not aware of the full reality of her home-life, are very proud of her. Her father is also very proud of her. He knows he wouldn't have been able to cope without her. He often brings her back expensive presents from abroad to show his gratitude and ease his guilt. He loves his children dearly but he cannot bear to be with his wife, especially when she is drinking. He doesn't see Katy's isolation or recognise the loss of her childhood: neither does her mum.

Coping with Double Messages

One of the most confusing matters for a child living in an alcoholic home is the delivery of many double messages that contradict each other. For a young person struggling to find some security, they add to the frightening instability in his life. I've listed three of the more common double messages coming from their disturbed parents that have perplexed many of the youngsters with whom I have worked.

Don't tell lies/ It is all right for us to lie about the drinking

Like many parents, the alcoholic and his partner plan to bring their children up to be honest and may be quite strict disciplinarians as far as telling the truth is concerned. Therefore, children are puzzled when they hear the alcoholic pleading with his partner to distort the truth to his boss; asking her to make excuses for his absence from work. Also, the promise, "I'll never touch a drop of alcohol again", is broken over and over. Children come to believe that the oath of, "Next time it will be different", is lying.

Even more disconcerting and alarming, is the fact that their parents are dishonest with them about the drinking. Many well-meaning parents are so enwrapped in their denial of the alcoholism that they cannot see that the children are observing quite accurately what is happening. In my experience the young people are the most aware. They know that Mum hasn't got 'flu' again; they can see that she is paralytic. However, they learn that the truth has very little meaning in an alcoholic household. Very quickly they understand that one of the ways to survive in this family is to cover up the reality of what is actually happening. Often, it is lying by omission; adopting the 'no-talking rule'. They are taught to cope the way their parents do — by keeping secrets. Coupled with this they learn not to trust; inside or outside the family.

You're not good enough/I can't cope with

Alcoholics tend to be perfectionists, expecting high sta .
themselves and others, judging with great censure if those e
tions aren't met. Many children of alcoholics wish that their par
had said, just once, "Well done. I'm proud of you. You're goo
enough the way you are." Usually, the response is something like,
"Why have you only got five 'As' and one 'B'. I expect a child of mine
to have six 'As'." Many children in these homes grow up believing
that no matter how hard they try they can do nothing well enough.
The start of the development of shame, a feeling of falling far short of
the mark.

Contradicting that message is the subtle but obvious communication that neither parent can cope with their lives; that they need at
least one of the children to provide some sort of order and stability in
the home. Some children may take on the role of parent in the family,
looking after the drinking parent, perhaps feeding him, putting him to
bed, clearing up after him. Also, they may care for the exhausted
caretaker, as well as the other younger people in the family. They may
take on responsibility for many of the household chores; cooking,
cleaning, shopping. In the meantime, they make sure that there is no
more conflict in the home by denying their own problems, their own
feelings.

If both parents are alcoholic, life is even less predictable, and
many young people live in this situation, surviving the best way they
know how. However, they feel trapped; the feeling is of having no
escape.

Although many work very hard, achieve many accomplishments,
several children of alcoholics never believe that they are good enough.
That message has been played over and over again. Sometimes it has
literally been knocked into them.

I love you/I haven't got time for you

Perhaps the most damaging double message is this one. Many
children of alcoholics hear this contradiction very clearly and struggle
to make sense of it.

The alcoholic, when sober, is often a wonderful parent to be
with. He is trying to ease his guilt about his out-of-control drinking by
being available and being fun; by buying expensive presents or taking

ɔn exciting trips. At this time, the children feel important ɔrted. However, within a short period, he is drinking, ent to their needs and feelings, shouting at them, perhaps even g violent towards them. The young people react with hurt nfusion.

Sometimes they are blamed by either parent for the drinking. Perhaps at times they just sense that their parents think it is their fault; nothing has been said. Quite often I am asked by youngsters, "Have I done something wrong? Is it because I've been naughty? Is it because I haven't done well at school? Is it because I haven't looked after my younger brothers or sisters well enough?" The underlying question which is rarely asked is, "Is it because I'm not lovable?"

With the non-alcoholic parent, the double message can be just as strong as that coming from the alcoholic. Sometimes her unspoken communication is stronger. Often, she is the less popular parent. At times, the alcoholic appears to make the effort to reform, but the caretaker is often miserable, irritable, nagging, depressed, tired and acting as though she carries the weight of the world on her shoulders. Although the caretaking parent may tell her children that she loves them, those observing her behaviour feel that they are in the way, that they are the cause of her unhappiness. Often, they see themselves as the reason for their parents' arguments. This conclusion is formed because no one takes the time or makes the effort to explain what the problem really is.

The Isolation of Children of Alcoholics

One of the reasons that the alcoholic and his partner are unaware of the effects of the illness of alcoholism on the young people in the family is because they don't know what is going on with their children. Their awareness and sensitivity have been blurred because they have been so obsessed with their particular addiction. Another explanation is that, as I mentioned in chapter three, many children of alcoholics look good on the surface. They learn to survive the chaos and insecurity by conforming, by being 'good' children, by not rocking the boat any more than it is already.

In this chapter we have already discussed how children of alcoholics learn not to talk about the drinking, and how not to trust others. Obviously, both these factors play a large part in them from others — inside and outside the family. What cont. even more to the loneliness is that these children learn that to normal, human emotions causes more stress than they can cope wit. They have learned that in their family it is not constructive to show feelings. When they have hurt, no one has noticed. When they have been pleased with an effort at school, they have been put down. When they have been angry, they have been punished.

Children raised in alcoholic families are intent on survival. They do whatever they can to bring stability and consistency into their lives. They will find ways that make it easier to cope and survive. As a result of not trusting others, they do not perceive their parents or siblings as resources for support. They live their lives, coping on their own. Feelings such as loneliness, anger, guilt, shame, anxiety and embarrassment lead to a state of depression, of desperation, of being overwhelmed. They cause pain and make it difficult to survive. As other family members are preoccupied with the addictions in the home, there is no one there to help them cope with those feelings. They learn to discount and repress them; they deal with life from a position of numbness.

The rules that I mentioned earlier in this book also contribute to the isolation of children from an alcoholic home. The unspoken regulations are formed for the sake of the survival of the family yet, paradoxically, contribute greatly to its breakdown. The most destructive rule for the children, as well as the adults is the 'No-Talking Rule'. The adherence to that law helps shut the child up within himself and accept that his thoughts, his questions, his feelings are not of importance. He cannot talk to his alcoholic parent about his observations, about his drinking, because to do so would threaten his delusion; he cannot talk to his non-alcoholic parent, because she is already letting it be known that she has too much to cope with; he cannot talk to his brothers and sisters because they have also learned the no-talking rule well. He cannot talk outside the family because he would be seen as being disloyal and letting the side down; then he'd cause more upset, and that has to be avoided at all costs. That's another rule.

Besides, he doesn't want his schoolmates to know what goes on at home. He'd been ever so embarrassed when he made the mistake of

.riend home to find that his mother had already been drinking
y that day. She slurred her speech, swayed as she walked. His
. had been there and explained that his Mum had once nursed
ɔroad and picked up a rare disease which made her behave strangely
at times. His friend had said nothing, so he didn't know whether he'd
guessed that Mum was actually drunk. He hasn't come back to visit
their family again.

Just recently, I was shown by Louise how profound the isolation
is for the child of an alcoholic when denial and blaming split the
family. Louise is twelve years old, the oldest of six children and the
daughter of an alcoholic vicar who has just found recovery. Her
mother brought her along to a group of 12 – 18 year olds I was
involved with; all children of alcoholics. Although the other young
people did their best to involve Louise in the group, by sharing their
experiences and feelings, she remained shy, withdrawn, hanging her
head and staring at the floor.

As it was a beautiful day, the group decided to have a break in the
activities and go for a walk. I was deep in conversation with one of the
other young people, when I became aware that Louise had placed
herself very close to me, matching her step with mine. I tried to
include her in the conversation, but, she refused to be drawn. She
continued to stay close. Sensing her desperation I moved away from
the group with her, searching in vain for some words that might help
her talk. After a long silence, she found the courage to blurt out, "My
Granny says my Daddy's drinking is my Mummy's fault. She says she
makes him do it."

Slowly, she began to talk about the conflict in the family that was
giving her so much pain. Granny, it seems, had a lot of power in the
family, although she lived more than two hundred miles away. She
had great problems in accepting that her only son, a pillar of the
Church, was alcoholic. From that distance, she tried to cover it up,
phoning regularly, trying to keep control of the situation. Louise's
mother was fraught, coping with six young children, between the ages
of six and twelve, an unpredictable alcoholic husband and trying to
hold the parish together. She looked exhausted when I met her.
Louise told me she often cried, especially when Granny had told her it
was her fault. Louise had tried to talk to her grandparents, but was
told she was too young to understand what was going on. Her

thoughts and feelings had been dismissed.

I realised that Louise was taking a huge risk by sharing with me about her family problems. Her grandmother would be furious, she said, because no one must know about her father's drinking. She anticipated that the older woman would attack her mother for being so disloyal as to suggest Louise needed some help.

That young girl saw it as her role in the family to be the strong one. She protected her younger brothers and sisters from knowing what was happening, she supported her mother emotionally, she had tried to stop her father's drinking, she had attempted to stop her grandmother's raging. Her function, as she saw it, was to keep the peace in the family. Yet, she ached with loneliness. She had no friends; she didn't have time to make them, and she couldn't take them home anyway because she would have been in danger of betraying the family secret.

The blindness, the passion for keeping that secret was destroying the love in that family. Fortunately, Louise has found the courage to defy her grandmother and has become involved with Alateen. Hopefully, she will find the love and acceptance there that she is so hungry for: the love and acceptance that has not been available in her fragmented family.

The Breaking of the Chain of Destruction

Children of alcoholics need and deserve help. So many are ignored, passed over and forgotten by so many people. They are innocent victims of their parents' addictions. Many learn behaviour patterns of surviving which may well help them cope with a traumatic childhood. Unless that pattern is broken they will go on to have greatly troubled and lonely adulthoods like their parents. If they have the physical predisposition, they are at risk of becoming alcoholics themselves. Alcoholism often runs in families, fifty to sixty per cent of all alcoholics have, or had, at least one alcoholic parent (see *It Will Never Happen to Me* by Claudia Black). Alternatively, they may continue the role they have been trained for in childhood — that of caretaker. They may be locked into a predetermined life-long pattern of having relationships with alcoholics or other needy people. Often, in adulthood, they develop emotional and/or psychological problems.

Help is available; unfortunately it is limited. Professionals in this country are just beginning to recognise the hazards of this large group of young people. Many have a lot to learn. Self-help groups such as Alateen and Adult Children of Alcoholics cater for the youngsters' needs. As yet, these groups are minimal in number. To find out if there is one in your area contact Al-Anon Headquarters. Their address can be found at the back of this book.

10

Adjusting to Recovering Parents

"Many said that they did not want any other parents; they only wanted a chance to know and to be understood by the parents they had."

The Forgotten Children, R. Margaret Cork

It is a common assumption that once the alcoholic starts recovery, the children will automatically 'come right'. To adopt such an attitude is yet another minimization of the devastating effects of alcoholism on the youngsters. It is also a denial of the fact that both adults are involved in a process of change that takes time. Indeed, many recovering alcoholics and caretakers find themselves growing up alongside their children. Early recovery is a time when adults are taking time to find out who they are. I have already described some of the changing roles within the family when adjusting to recovery (see chapter six). In these next pages I'd like to point out that young people also have great difficulty in coping with the changing roles.

In this chapter, one very important factor to remember is that children of alcoholics have rarely learned to communicate their needs or their feelings. The changes within the family as the adults recover can often leave them feeling frightened, taken for granted, resentful, perplexed, abandoned, rejected or left behind. Usually, because of their history they are unable to express that. Some feel very guilty because their feelings aren't of pure gratitude for one or both parents' recovery.

Although in time, recovery may bring some contented togetherness in the family, the young people, like their parents, are often shocked to find themselves facing a period of grief, of loss. The following is a list of major losses described to me by the young people I have worked with.

Loss of a Dream

During the drinking days, one of the ways that a lot of young people learn to survive, is to have a fantasy of what family life would be like if the alcoholic wasn't drinking. They conjure up and grimly hang on to an illusion of perfection. Usually, because of the extent of the chaos and pain surrounding the drinker, the child's dream is based on unrealistically high expectations of contented family life. Often, the vision is similar to a television soap opera.

The recovery of the parent brings disillusionment, because it is rarely accompanied by an immediate reality of 'happy families'. If the alcoholic and his relatives do go through an exciting honeymoon period, a painful adjusting period usually follows fast on its heels. Conflict, arguments, anger, aggression and sulking sometimes accompany the abstinence of the drinker, as they all jockey for position in the changing dynamics within the family.

Sometimes the dream is shattered because, although the alcoholic stops drinking, the parents still do not get on together. Then the family has to cope with the break-up of the marriage after the drinking days are over. That can produce a lot of resentment.

Stan's father has been in recovery for four years. He is a busy doctor. In his spare time he appears to have a mission to help other alcoholics. Stan's mum is as devoted to helping the partners of alcoholics. The young lad, who is 14 years old, is lonely. The only thing that is different is that his dad is not drinking. Stan still feels left out. His dream of family togetherness has not materialized. When asked if he had told his parents how he felt, he said he thought it disloyal to do so.

Loss of the Old, Familiar Rules and Roles

The loss of the rules mentioned in chapter four is a painful experience for any adult. For children, it can be devastating because those rules have been the foundation of their lives, the way they have learned to exist and survive in the family. Indeed, if the alcoholic has been drinking all of their young lives, the rules of how to live with an out-of-control drinker and his angry, frightened family are all they know about survival. Some adults have had other types of close relationships in their history; many children of alcoholics have not.

Recovery brings the loss of the old, terrible, yet familiar life-style that the children had learned to cope with and knew which role to play to feel safer. At all costs, they knew that no matter how much pain the alcoholic brought to the family, he had to be protected. They were aware at some level of their consciousness that his drinking was what the family primarily focussed on and revolved around. They also accepted that the role of the caretaking parent was to be uptight, angry and preoccupied.

Both parents have started to change. The alcoholic isn't drinking. How do they react to him? Will it last? Do they trust him? The caretaker is gradually becoming more relaxed. How do they react to her? Will it last? Do they trust her?

Sadly, because of the obsession of both parents with their alternate addictions and their lack of awareness, the children suffer greatly. This can continue into the period of recovery, as both parents become just as preoccupied in coping with their changing attitudes, as well as their grief. Often, because the parents are so involved with their own healing, they cannot see the difficulties their children are having in adjusting to the alterations within the family.

The Loss of the Role as Parent

Theresa was sixteen years old. During her father's drinking days she looked after him, went searching for him when he disappeared, tried to sober him up, nursed his hangovers and generally kept an eye on him. Mum coped with Dad's drinking by shutting out reality and going to bed. Often she wouldn't emerge from the bedroom for days at a time. Theresa would cook her meals and care for her. Both parents owned a small fruit and vegetable shop. On her parents 'bad days', Theresa ran the business very competently. She was admired by many for her efficiency and ability to cope with unexpected problems.

I met this young lady eighteen months after her father started to recover from his alcoholism. She was very depressed. Gradually, over time, Theresa admitted to resenting her father's recovery, because she felt she had been used and cast aside; she believed she was needed no longer.

Dad, in his enthusiasm for recovery, and a new way of life, had thrown himself back into building up his business. He kept telling Theresa to go away and enjoy herself, not realising that she didn't know how to. Her self-esteem had been based on the fact that she felt valued and important in the drinking days: now she felt diminished. Mum had also stopped hiding in bed and became involved in the shop. Her parents seemed to be getting close again and the young girl felt left out, rejected.

Theresa's way of shouting for help was to slash her wrists with a razor. Fortunately, the cuts weren't deep, but the crisis brought her mother and father to recognise that she needed help. Slowly, with counselling, she started communicating her feelings with her shocked parents. Both had been oblivious to the effects of their behaviour on their daughter. In time, they worked out a system where they shared responsibility for the shop. More importantly, with the help of A.A., Al-Anon, Alateen and some more counselling, they began to repair and heal their relationships with each other. Theresa started to learn that she was loved for who she was — not what she did.

Theresa's story is not an unusual one in families where there are recovering parents. Children who have become the mainstays of the family in the drinking days, who have parented their parents, find it very difficult to cope with being insensitively relegated to the role of child in the family. The reversal of positions has to be done gently, slowly and with much open discussion if it is going to work without causing more emotional damage to the young people.

The Loss of Role as Emotional Partner

Jack is fourteen years old. He is the only child in the family. Until recently, he had a very close emotional bond with his mother. When his father was drinking, Jack was seen by himself and his mother as 'the man in the house'. Jack's father often disappeared for days or weeks at a time, so the young lad was used to doing a lot of the heavy work around the house as well as providing a shoulder for his mother to cry on. She often said she would never have been able to cope without him. He was such a reliable young man.

In the last six months, Jack's excellent school record had been blemished because he had failed a number of exams, mainly because he hadn't worked for them. He had been playing truant and had two shoplifting charges to face. When I met her, his mother was puzzled about his behaviour. She thought family life had improved greatly in the two years that Jack's father had been in recovery. She had been surprised at Jack's withdrawn sulkiness, but had put it down to adolescent moodiness.

Initially, I found Jack very difficult to talk to. Although he had agreed to see me, he was sullen and refused to make any effort to communicate with me. After a couple of meetings, we terminated our contract because I saw no point in trying to help him if he wasn't ready to help himself. After six months, he came to see me again, after another shop-lifting incident. This time the rage was bursting out of him and he told me that he "hated the bastard". It became clear that it was his father he was describing. He saw him stealing his role in the family and his relationship with his mother. Jack also had a lot of rage at his mum for being "so soft" with his father. Why was she so nice to him after all the pain he had caused when he was drinking? Who the hell did he think he was, telling him what to do? After all, Jack had run the house when his father was "pissed out of his mind". Why did she let him boss Jack about? Hadn't he looked after her when his father was messing around with other women? Why was she ignoring Jack now and giving the old man the attention?

According to Jack, his father continued to have some very rigid attitudes towards his son. There seemed to be quite a lot of competition between the two males. His mother appeared unable to reach out and bridge the growing gap that separated her from her son.

As yet, the young lad has not been able to resolve his pain. He is still acting out his rage, still getting into trouble with the law. I hear on the grapevine that he has been getting involved in heavy drinking. He has dropped his counselling session.

The Need for Help and Support for Children of Recovering Alcoholics

On re-reading this chapter, I feel heavy and sad. It paints a black picture of recovery for children from these backgrounds. Yet, it is part of the reality that my colleagues and I work with. The children in an alcoholic family can continue to be the hidden victims long after their parents find recovery. Frequently, the adults are not ready to give the younger people the emotional support they need at this crucial time; they are too involved in their own painful struggles in healing from the devastations of this illness. Perhaps, too, they are hampered by their guilt and shame about damaging behaviour during the drinking days. Disciplining can be sporadic and inconsistent in early recovery. Defining boundaries around what is and is not acceptable behaviour for the children is difficult if the adults don't know who they themselves are and what stance feels right for them. Many parents need assistance in learning parenting skills when they start to get well.

The good news is that there is help available. Alateen and Adult Children of Alcoholics groups provide support for young people coping with their parents' recovery from the addiction. The programme gives them a fellowship to lean on while their parents are not fully available to them. It also shows the ways that they can seek help for themselves and make some changes within themselves so that they are better able to cope with life — not just gritting their teeth and surviving. Love, understanding, acceptance and acknowledgement of their importance as individuals in their own right are important factors of the healing processes in these groups.

Some alcoholism treatment centres also provide support for the children of the alcoholic. Farm Place, near Dorking, is one of these.

11

Adult Children of Alcoholics

"With the help of parents, other authority figures and institutions (such as education, organized religion, politics, the media and even psychotherapy) most of us learn to stifle and deny our child within. When this vital part of us is not nurtured and allowed freedom of expression, a false or codependent self emerges."

Healing the Child Within, Charles L. Whitfield

Bobby is a well-respected doctor. He is thirty-eight years old, single and very popular with the ladies. His mother, sister and brother are all recovering alcoholics. Bobby was also addicted to drugs and alcohol and has been in recovery for ten years. He has one sister who does not appear to have a problem with being addicted to mood-altering chemicals.

In his childhood, Bobby was very lonely. His mother was often drunk or hiding in her room and his father, whom he describes as Victorian in his attitudes towards children, was rarely at home. When he was, the children were terrified of him because he was often angry. Their achievements at school or around the house were never good enough.

On the surface, this young man looks as though he has done well with his life, particularly in the last ten years. His career is very successful and he appears to have a lot of friends. Recently, Bobby sought professional help because his loneliness had become quite profound.

Although there were a lot of people around in his life, he felt that he didn't have any meaningful relationships. He admitted that he had cultivated a charming persona to manipulate people into liking him; as a result, he never felt accepted, never felt valued for who he really was. He had a long string of girlfriends, but he recognised that he was trapped into a pattern of relating to them in a way that left him feeling even more isolated. Bobby enjoyed the chase, he liked pursuing the women that he was attracted to and winning them over. However, as soon as they started to get close, to get to know Bobby, he panicked and opted out of the relationship.

Bobby has a lot of shame. His flirtatious nature hides a lot of anger. Some of that anger is at other people, but much of it is directed at himself because he does not believe that he is worth loving. He does not see himself as good enough. That message was drummed into him over and over again in childhood.

Kathleen is forty-two years old and was married once, very briefly (six months) to someone who was alcoholic. She has been a teacher. Recently, she has given up her job because she is exhausted. That draining of energy happened over the years, because she has devoted all of her life to looking after other people and has not had her needs fulfilled. Until she hit this period of crisis she did not know how to ask for help for herself. Indeed, until she hurt enough, she wasn't aware that she needed help.

This woman also grew up in an alcoholic home. Her father was the drinker. There were five children in the family. Kathleen was the middle one. Dad was often unemployed and the family had to struggle through long periods of poverty which were made worse because food-money often disappeared for the purchasing of alcohol. Kathleen's father was often violent and frightening. She saw that her mission in life was to make her mother happy. As a child, she was aware of the older woman's misery and strove to lighten her load. As the only girl in the family, she took on the role of substitute mum and encouraged her brothers to come to her with their problems. There was a rule that Mum mustn't be worried. That role of protecting Mother has continued to this day despite the fact that the older woman still worries, still is miserable.

The real problem is that Kathleen has never been free to be herself. She has tried to be super-woman, pleasing everyone else and looking after their happiness. She has denied and repressed her rage, bitterness, grief and resentments behind a bright smile. Keeping up that act has cost her. It was the only way that she knew how to survive, but her incredible strength was eventually sapped and she collapsed with exhaustion.

In the last few years, a new self-help group has emerged in this country, Adult Children of Alcoholics (A.C.O.A.). There is a large group of people who have special needs because they live in a great deal of emotional agony and isolation. That pain comes from years of smothering their feelings and suppressing their true selves. Children of alcoholics, like other people who have grown up in troubled homes, do not know who they are. They have not been allowed or encouraged to discover their uniqueness. As they progress into adulthood, they continue to practise the patterns of behaviour which helped them survive in their family of origin. Fear is often the centre of their lives and that produces a rigidity of personality. The drive is for perfection: the need to prove that I am in control and one step ahead of everyone else. Feelings continue to be stifled, and the loneliness that started in childhood becomes overwhelming with advancing years.

The group of A.C.O.A. provides a necessarily safe place where one can meet with people who have grown up in similar homes; who have lived with the same isolation, oppression and neglect; who are all desperately trying to seek relief from the pain; who want to be accepted for who they are and not the image they are striving to portray. The self-help group helps reduce that overpowering loneliness.

Using the Rules to Survive

In chapter three, I listed the rules that many families of alcoholics adopt in order to cope with the chaos caused by the behaviour of the alcoholic. For the children these regulations become a way of survival because they provide some kind of security and stability in the home. They help to stop the boat from rocking too much. However, they also encourage a denial of the uniqueness and creativity of each individual in the family. Although most adult children of alcoholics look good and are usually successful in their chosen careers, that denial of themselves continues into later life, because they are still following the pattern of coping and relating to others that commenced in childhood; following the rules that their parents taught them. In the heads of many adult children the rules are translated into the following list.

— Always be good.

— Don't argue. Be seen and not heard.

— Don't show your feelings; they are not important.

— Don't get angry or upset.

— Always be in control. Don't show your vulnerabilities.

— Always look good.

— Don't rock the boat. Avoid conflict.

— Achieving is what earns you love — so do well in school, at work.

— Even if it means hurting yourself — never betray the family secret.

— Don't talk about the drinking.

— No one is more important than the alcoholic. Your function in life is to look after him or some similarly needy person.

— Always maintain the status quo.

— Don't question, just follow the rules.

These principles run many adult children's lives and allow for no flexibility. In seeking close intimate relationships in adulthood, they cause many problems because to be genuinely intimate is to accept and be accepted as an imperfect human being. To genuinely love and be loved requires breaking every one of the rules. Spontaneity, self-nurturing, having fun, finding the courage and freedom to be are not part of the lives of many adult children of alcoholics unless they have received help in coming to terms with themselves. When such people are not loved in the way they want to be loved, they do what they did to earn the approval of their parents — they compulsively lock into the drive of achieving all of the above goals: with perfection. Thus, avoiding what they have never had and are eagerly seeking: real closeness with another human being. Shame and fear of abandonment have taken over, blocking them off from others.

Often, the only way to continue obeying the rules and find some kind of close relationship is to seek out another addict. This is one of the reasons why a large number of children of alcoholics end up marrying or cohabiting with another alcoholic or even a succession of addicted people. Sometimes this happens despite the individual's best intentions to stay away from such a relationship.

Problems that Many A.C.O.A.'s find in Close Relationships

As a result of being brought up in a disturbed family, many adult children find they do not know how to relate 'normally' to other people. Coupled with this, the expectations of what a relationship should be are usually very unrealistic.

Many adults who had an alcoholic parent risk addiction themselves. If you suspect that this is the case for you, my recommendation is that you get help with your drinking problem first before you try and sort out your relationship problems. Dependence on alcohol clouds and distorts many issues.

The following are some of the relationship problems of people of all ages who are children of alcoholics. Much of the pain results from fear.

The Fear of Conflict

Arguments are something that children of alcoholics have grown up with. Perhaps those arguments even became violent at times. The rage that exists in an alcoholic environment is rarely resolved. Many children growing up in these families learn not to be angry, because to do so adds more tension to the already strained atmosphere. Instead, because they repress the feeling, they can become depressed and even have suicidal thoughts. Others are frightened of their anger because every so often the pressure is no longer containable and it erupts as rage. There is often terror at the strength of this feeling — a fear that they might hurt someone.

Dealing with another person's anger is also difficult, especially if it is being directed at them. For adult children, anger is often synonymous with rejection. The attitude is, "If you are angry with me that means you don't love me and therefore you are going to leave me". Many people who are raised in alcoholic homes won't show their anger for that reason: in case the other person feels rejected or abandoned.

Because people in alcoholic families don't discuss feelings, usually children of alcoholics don't know how to resolve their anger, don't know how to dispel it. They are not aware that anger needs to be recognised, acknowledged, discussed, understood and consequently dissipated. Most healthy relationships will contain times when people disagree, get irritated by the other. Conflict is healthy: people grow and mature as they work through it.

The Fear of Loss of Control

Frequently, people who feel out of control are obsessed with the need to control. This happens for many children of alcoholics. The fear is, "If I am not in control, always, then everything will fall apart". This lesson was learned at a very young age. In an alcoholic family, it often feels that everything is crumbling, and the most successful way to feel safe and survive is to try and arrange some control over the chaos.

In adult relationships that need to control often continues because of the fear of being dependent. The belief is, "If I relax and let him help me, I might like it. I need to be prepared for the fact that he might let me down some time and if I have lost my independence I might be devastated." Adult children spend a lot of time in relationships, looking over their shoulders, anticipating the inevitable abandonment, frightened that when the rejection does come, they won't be able to cope. They are caught in a fearful double-edged battle, because in struggling to maintain the control, they actually lose it. Although they strive to appear extremely independent, in fact, what they are desperately wanting is the belief that the other is really there for them. The fear of being deserted is overwhelming. History has taught them that people they loved (the alcoholic and partner) were rarely there for them, emotionally. Learning to trust that history will not always repeat itself takes a lot of faith and trust. This fear can be eased with discussion, time and patience on the part of both persons in the current relationship.

The Fear of Losing The Self

This fear is present because children of alcoholics never really establish who they are when they are growing up. Instead of developing a sense of self they become what the environment, or the mood of the alcoholic or caretaker, required at the time. As a result, children of alcoholics rarely learn to trust their inner feelings or instincts. They learn to survive by trying to please other people.

Decision-making can be threatening to adult children, especially if they have been trying to be their own person. The security found in pleasing other people can be very tempting, but can also be threatening if the individual fears being taken over or engulfed. It takes time and hard work to learn to stand on one's own ground and be comfortable with making decisions and even saying 'No' to another. Self-confidence grows with valuing one's own responses, perceptions and opinions; also choosing to be with other people who hold that person in esteem.

The Fear of Being Found Out

Many adult children have been acting a role all of their lives. Their shame is very profound, because they have been driven to seek perfection and never attained it. They did not have the security in childhood of knowing that they were loved for who they were. Instead, they worked very hard at trying to keep their parents happy, desperately trying to earn love and somehow always feeling that they had fallen short of the mark.

Quite often, they were overtly and covertly blamed for the trauma in the family. As a result many such children grow up believing at some level that there is an evil or dark side to them that will overwhelm them if it is not kept in check. Therefore, intimacy with another becomes threatening because that frightening negative side might be exposed.

Because adult children are excruciatingly self-critical, they believe that others will also judge and condemn them in the same way. As a result, they keep running towards that goal of perfection hoping that it will find them love. Yet, when they *are* loved they never really believe it because they know they have been false, not true to themselves.

The only way to cope with this problem is to learn to face one's shame; face the darkness and accept it as part of one's self (as described in chapter seven). When a person finds peace with himself then there is no longer a fear of being found out.

The Fear of Defining Boundaries in Relationships

Children of alcoholics grow up in a very confused world. The alcoholism causes so much chaos that the boundaries of each individual become very blurred. Sometimes is was difficult to know who was the child and who was the parent, who was taking the responsible role, and who was taking the irresponsible one. Sometimes, it became so confusing that it was difficult to know who was feeling whose pain. Was it mine? Was it my mother's pain? Was it my father's? Frequently, privacy can be invaded in such a home and there is a lot of insensitivity about who owns what. For example, the alcoholic may be gasping for a drink and having no money helps himself to the housekeeping, the contents of his children's piggy bank or the small change in his wife's purse. Often, children of alcoholics are unaware of limitations in social behaviour, of what is appropriate or not.

This confusion can continue on into adulthood. Caretakers who have grown up tidying up after others can be upset if another becomes indignant about having had their room cleaned up for them. Controllers can be rebuffed when they insist on paying the full bill for a meal when the others have agreed to 'go Dutch'. One partner in a new relationship can feel overwhelmed if the other moves in too close, too quickly. These, of course, happen in relationships where there has been no alcoholism in the family. However, many people will discuss and negotiate boundaries as they get to know each other better. They learn that different people need differing amounts of space. They have developed skills for doing so in their family of origin. Some children of alcoholics do not know how to negotiate these boundaries in relationships, because they have missed out on that experience in childhood. As a result, some can feel overwhelmed by others; others are overwhelming in their relationships.

The Fear of Having Fun

Spontaneous play and laughter can often be missing in the childhood of someone whose parent is alcoholic. If it is present, the drinker can 'go over the top' with his behaviour and becomes frightening and insensitively teasing. Recurrently, adults who have been raised in such a family find themselves too intense, too cautious. To relax, let go and spontaneously have fun can be seen as losing control. Often that energy is curbed because there is a fear that, if the defences are let down too far, then the next crisis might creep up from behind without warning. Many adult children feel they have to be 'on guard' all the time.

The Fear of Commitment

Adult children of alcoholics place very high expectations on themselves. As a result, they very rarely succeed in what they are trying to achieve, whether it is a work project, a hobby or a relationship. Adult children are used to failing — as they see it. Because they tend to judge situations as black or white, never grey, what they have done is either a failure or a success; rarely the latter. As a result, relationships are often doomed to failure because they eagerly go headlong into them making a great deal of emotional investment. Initially, the other partner can be flattered by this, but later can be overwhelmed by the intensity of the feeling and may retreat. Many adult children will interpret this action as rejection and see themselves as failing. Frequently, the reaction is to withdraw the commitment very quickly. It takes time to learn that a relationship is a gradual process and both partners commit themselves slowly. It grows according to what both people put into it.

The Fear of Being Vulnerable

To be vulnerable is to open ourselves up and let someone in close. Children of alcoholics have survived by doing just the opposite; by building strong defensive walls that are difficult to penetrate. To let those defences down is frightening, because that brings a fear of the loss of self and a terror of being overwhelmed or overpowered by some other person. Quite often in childhood, when that protection was missing, the sensation of being taken over by either parent was devastating. This is particularly true if either of the adults was violent.

Adult children are in a tug-of-war because, in order to have a close, intimate relationship, they have to become vulnerable to one other person. History has taught them that that can be a negative experience. It takes a lot of courage to discover that by lowering these barriers, being vulnerable can sometimes have positive results.

The Aftermath of Incest

Many children of alcoholics have had to cope with an incestuous relationship. Although incest does not occur in every family system where alcoholism is present, it happens frequently enough to be given a space for discussion in this chapter.

Incest can happen between mothers and sons, fathers and sons, brothers and sisters, but the most common incestuous relationship is between father and daughter. It can be overt or covert. Overt incest involves sexual contact within the family. It can take the form of intercourse, but the most usual forms involve masturbation, the fondling of breasts and genitals.

Marie was in treatment for her alcoholism when she was thirty. It wasn't until she was about to leave that programme that she found the courage to talk for the first time in her life about her incestuous relationship with her alcoholic father. It started when she was eight years old and finished when she ran away from home at fifteen. When asked why she had never told her mother she replied, "What good would it have done? My father would have hit me or hit her. She couldn't have stopped it." Marie felt she could talk to no one about it. Even as she found the courage to share it as a mature woman, she was surprised that she was not blamed or seen as disgusting.

Her subsequent sexual relationships didn't last for long. She had great problems in trusting men. Her anger at her father was projected onto any brave man who tried to get close to her. Marie needed and received long-term counselling from someone who specialized in helping those with problems of sexual abuse.

Covert incest is much more subtle; it does not involve physical contact. In such a relationship the father treats the girl like his 'little princess', an emotional substitute for his wife. This can often happen in an alcoholic home where there is no longer an emotional bond between the parents. Father can be jealous of his daughter's boyfriends. This young lady does not feel abused, she feels idealized.

She can also idealize her father and finds great difficulty in breaking away from that bonding because he made her feel so special. As a result, in her eyes, her father was the ideal love object, therefore she spends the rest of her life seeking out men who are just like him. This can be a very powerful relationship and pattern to try and break away from; the pain of changing can be agonizing.

'Coming out' about either kind of incestuous relationship takes a great deal of courage. It means breaking a family secret which seems like being disloyal to the parent who was involved. However, the damage of incest goes deep — even deeper than the damage of living with alcoholism. There is good, specialized, professional help available (please see back of the book). If you have such a problem, you may be relieved to find that you are not alone. Many others have been through what you have lived with — and a good number have gone on to have fulfilling relationships — after they have received help.

Healing of Adult Children of Alcoholics

Many adults who grew up in an alcoholic environment are in a great deal of emotional pain and have difficult problems with intimate relationships. Many have a profound shame, a feeling of not being good enough, just as described in chapter seven. Others have a great sense of loss because they didn't have a childhood where they could play like other children, cry, have tantrums, have friends, and have stable, reliable parents like other children. Quite rightly, they feel they had to grow up too quickly and become responsible too soon. Several become 'parents' long before their time.

One of the most difficult feelings for many children of alcoholics to admit to is the rage they feel towards their parents. Often this feeling is turned inward and allowed to fester because the children (of all ages) are being so responsible, so reasonable, so good. Thoughts like the following can submerge the anger: "I can't be angry at my parents because they were coping in the best way they knew how", "Of course I'm not angry at my mother. She's alcoholic, so she's sick. How can I possibly be angry with her?" Indeed, these issues are often true. Alcoholic and caretaking parents do cope in the best way they know how with a very destructive and devastating illness and it is rare that they hurt their children intentionally. Also, it is a fact, alcoholics are sick.

However, the point is that unless children of alcoholics can surface that anger, it can cause health problems, stunt creativity and destroy relationships. In order to become their true selves, they need an outlet to express that rage and massive feeling of loss. Obviously, it is better not to give vent to that grief within the family. Relatives either have too much invested interest in keeping the status quo, or too much guilt of their own and can't give the solid, objective empathy that an adult child needs when he or she begins to release those feelings.

Many children of alcoholics need professional therapeutic help; others find relief in sharing with other A.C.O.A.'s and finding a common life experience. Telling one's story, recognizing the patterns of relationship, letting go of feelings, and learning to forgive are all vital parts of the healing process. It is very important that those feelings are accepted and not dismissed as wrong.

As the grief, shame, and rage are expressed and discussed it becomes easier to release the pain and stand back from it. In observing the patterns of one's life there is a gradual release of tension, a realisation of one's own individual power, an acceptance that it is no longer necessary to tolerate being mistreated. There are choices about what kind of relationships we become involved in. We can change ourselves.

It takes time to recover from being an adult child of an alcoholic. The mold of denying the reality of oneself was cast a long time ago. A lot of hard work and patience needs to be invested before you can break out of it. However, when that does happen, the rewards are enormous. Adult children of alcoholics can find the Freedom to Be: and the Right to Be.

12

Love and Alcoholism

"I define love thus: the will to extend one's self for the purpose of nurturing one's own or another's spiritual growth."

The Road Less Travelled, M. Scott Peck

I believe that this concluding chapter describes the essence of what this book is really about. Love and Alcoholism: positive and negative spirituality: a quest for wholeness as a human being. Yet, I struggle with a great reluctance to write about it. Partly because love and spirituality are such vast subjects they are almost impossible to define; they are both so personal and experiential. One has to be acquainted with both to know that they are a fundamental part of our lives and closely related to each other. Nevertheless, the perceptions and sensations of the experiences of different people vary greatly.

Many correlate the term spirituality with religion, and then panic because the fear is that they are being advised to become 'Holy Joes' or 'religious fanatics'. However, I have met many spiritual people who are not religious, who choose to remain outside the dogma of organised religion. On the other hand, I have come across many religious people who are not spiritually oriented. I know several who have integrated their spirituality with what they have learned in the church, synagogue or temple. One's spirituality *may* include organized religion but can often transcend it.

Actually, spirituality has to do with the quality of one's relationship with oneself, with others and with the world around us. It is a mistake to assume that we have to believe in God to be spiritual. He is one possible spiritual focus. Our spirituality develops around who or what is the most important focus in our lives: who or what takes up most of our time and energy. Spirituality is part of being human, an essential element of the nature of mankind; as are the other necessary physical and emotional ingredients.

Spirituality can be a negative or positive force. We can choose to go either way. The vortex of the whirlwind of energy that is negative spirituality is fear. That emotion petrifies; the sufferer tries to diminish the intensity of the terror by trying to control life and predict what might be the outcome. As a result, he or she feels isolated, disconnected, separate, alone, fragmented, unloved and unlovable. Negative spirituality attracts negative experiences. People whose lives are dominated by fear often have health and relationship problems. They allow past painful experiences to influence their attitudes about the future. Worrying creates a vicious circle of being frightened which makes the fearful person rigid and inflexible, unable to be spontaneous or to flow with the current of Life. As a result, they are denying their own potential, repressing their own reality and getting pulled down into a dark pit of depression and inertia.

On the other hand, positive spirituality has as its axis Love or peace of mind: accepting ourselves, and others, as they really are, without the need to change or control them. People who are focussed on their positive spirituality accept that it is in changing ourselves, our thoughts, our feelings, our behaviours that we find peace of mind. Our wholeness does not come from trying to fix others. Positive spirituality attracts positive experiences. Those who have found serenity enjoy good health and warm, loving relationships. They love the potential in things, trusting life, change, and love. Their vulnerability is their greatest strength. They have a strong sense of self and can love and let go.

Being human means being imperfect. Few people, if any, achieve positive spirituality all of the time. Many move backwards and forwards between the negative and positive. Those who are in emotional, mental and sometimes physical pain have chosen predominantly to move with the negative spiritual energy. This includes many alcoholics and their suffering relatives.

Carl Jung, the renowned psychologist, described alcoholism as the, "Spiritual thirst of our being for wholeness". This quotation came from a letter that he wrote to Bill W., one of the co-founders of Alcoholics Anonymous. Feeling whole or complete is a basic human need. This makes it easier to understand why someone can make alcohol his 'god' — which is what happens when that person develops this illness. Ask any recovering addicted drinker what he or she was searching for in the bottle and the reply will be an overwhelming need for that feeling of contentment that he initially received from the alcohol. That intoxicating liquid has become a panacea for all ills; it overcomes feelings of shyness, by relaxing the individual, helping him become more outgoing and less self-conscious; it peps up a person when she is feeling depressed or unhappy; it settles feelings of upset, anger, fear or resentments — for the time being. As the illness takes hold and progresses, it becomes more and more necessary to drink alcohol in order to feel 'normal'. The spiritual journey that develops into alcoholism probably began as a search for happiness or contentedness. However, alcohol provides a negative spirituality. Making that seductive liquid the focus of one's life puts the seeker on a destructive, descending spiral which pulls him or her closer and closer to darkness, isolation and death.

The positive side of compulsive addictive behaviour is that it eventually leads to terrible crises which can cause enough pain to push the individual to shift the emphasis towards asking for help. This, therefore, can break the isolation and start the process of a search for a healthy spiritual focus. Recovery from alcoholism becomes an upward journey of discovery and healing which is actually a spiritual quest. The programme and fellowship of Alcoholics Anonymous provide a strong foundation for building a positive spirituality. One way to find wholeness is to reach out and share with others how we are feeling. Positive spirituality comes from accepting the unconditional love of a self-help group, counsellor or trusted friend; it comes from being accepted for who we are. Love is healing; it can take years of receiving such love to recover and stay recovering from the devastation of alcoholism.

It is a similar pattern for many addicted caretakers, whether they are the adults or children in the family. The most important focus for family members has become the drinking alcoholic and his erratic behaviour. The more the family becomes obsessed with the alcoholic and trying to fix him, the more they become caught up in a downward spiral of negative spirituality. Fear is the issue that dominates their lives. Where fear is in control, love is stifled. As the illness progresses, the balance in the family shifts and more and more emphasis is placed on maintaining control. It is done to try and provide a feeling of security, but what this attitude and behaviour does is to destroy. The destruction affects the alcoholic, the caretaker and the children. The addicted drinker is cushioned from reality by the protectiveness of the family; thus, he is stopped from feeling the pain produced by the crises and denied the right to change direction and choose recovery. The partner, in her efforts to control, becomes obsessed and preoccupied, stunting her own growth as a human being as she denies her feelings, the reality of herself. The children grow up in an atmosphere where they do not have the freedom to discover who they are and they learn to cope with life by acting out a false role. In an alcoholic home, the accent is not on spiritual growth but on the repression of the individual. Often, control becomes more important than the valuing of one's self.

However, the crises that happen in the family can become a 'gift'. The danger, the pain can become severe enough to produce an opportunity for change. It only takes one person to discover a positive way of life and the dynamics, the balance within the family can follow suit. The spirituality within that group can change from negative to positive as the rage, grief, pain, and shame are allowed to find outlets for expression; as the shackles of control are released and each individual finds the freedom to be his or her own self; as they begin to trust life as a process with which they want to flow, not keep in check; as they 'open up', individuals within the family seek help elsewhere. Healing can be found in the unconditional love and acceptance that come from groups such as Al-Anon, Alateen and Adult Children of Alcoholics.

Sometimes, that healing has to come separately. Perhaps the alcoholic continues to drink. This does not mean that family members cannot find peace of mind. Sometimes, the alcoholic recovers and yet his family do not. It takes a powerful love to say, "I can no longer stay in this situation. To do so would be destructive. I care about you, but I need to move away."

When alcoholics and their close ones become prepared over time "To extend themselves for the purpose of nurturing their own or another's spiritual growth" (M. Scott Peck), then respect and love grow within the family. Along with this comes a deepening of compassion, an acceptance and valuing of each individual self, as well as a high regard for the other's uniqueness and separateness. Love, which both accepts and encourages healthy growth in the other, also heals. Caretaking which is rooted in fear, is possessive or dependent, can be destructive.

Newcomers and strangers to the self-help groups of A.A. or Al-Anon are often shocked to hear comments like, "I am glad I am an alcoholic", or, "If my partner had not been alcoholic, I would never have found Al-Anon and never found this serenity, this peacefulness". Such people are recognizing and acknowledging that the years of pain, chaos and destruction have a profound value. Without hitting that 'rock bottom' they would not have recognized the need to find a new way of life. They would not have appreciated the presence of a healing love. They would not have discovered a sense of wholeness. They would have been unaware of the energy that is their own unconditional love which pushes them to reach out and help others, and play their own role as part of the universe.

They have come to know and value the meaning of the words of the following evangelical hymn.

> Amazing grace! How sweet the sound
> That saved a wretch like me!
> I once was lost, but now am found,
> Was blind, but now I see.
>
> 'Twas grace that taught my heart to fear,
> And grace my fears relieved;
> How precious did that grace appear
> The hour I first believed!
>
> Through many dangers, toils and snares,
> I have already come;
> 'Tis grace hath brought me safe thus far,
> And grace will lead me home.

Amazing Grace, John Newton

To many, this describes the essence of the miracle of recovery from alcoholism. The healing of both the alcoholic and those close to him or her; the freeing of each so that they can choose to experience the joy of their uniqueness. That is Freedom from the Bottle.

Recommended Reading

Anonymous: *Twenty-four hours a day*, Hazelden Fndtn.
Beattie, Melodie: *Codependent No More*, 1987, Hazelden Fndtn.
Black, Claudia: *It Will Never Happen to Me*, 1981, Ballentine
Bradshaw, John: *Bradshaw on: The Family*, 1988, Health Communications
Cutland, Liz: *Kick Heroin*, 1985, Gateway
Ditzler, Joyce & James: *Coming off Drink*, 1987 Papermac
Ditzler, Joyce & James: *If You Really Loved Me*, 1989, Papermac
Fossum & Mason: *Facing Shame, Families in Recovery*, 1986, Norton
Geringer, Woititz: *Adult Children of Alcoholics*, 1983, Health Communications
Heilman, Richard: *Easy Recognition of Alcoholism and Drug Dependence*, Hazelden Fndtn.
Jampolsky, E. J.: *Love is Letting Go of Fear*, 1981, Celestial Arts
Jung, Carl: *Letters* Vol 2 (1951–1961) pp. 623–625
Kopp, Sheldon B.: *If You Meet the Buddha on the Road, Kill Him!*, 1976, Bantam
Kurtz, Ernest: *Shame and Guilt: Characteristics of the Dependency Cycle*, 1981, Hazelden Fndtn.
Laing, R. D.: *Knots*, 1972, Penguin
Norwood, Robin: *Women who Love too Much*, 1986, Arrow
Scott Peck, M.: *The Road less Travelled*, 1987, Rider
Whitfield, Charles, L.: *Healing the Child Within*, 1987, Health Communications
Woodman, Marion: *Addiction to Perfection*, 1980, Inner City

Books from the Support Organisations

Al-Anon: *Twelve Steps and Traditions*
          The Dilemma of the Alcoholic Marriage
          One Day at a Time in Alanon
Alateen: *Hope for Children of Alcoholics*
Alcoholics Anonymous: *The Big Book*
          The Twelve Steps and Traditions
          (Addresses below)

The Treatment Centre referred to in this book is

Farm Place
Ockley
Surrey
RH5 5NG
Tel: 030679 742

it helps the families of alcoholics as well as the primary sufferers themselves.

Self-Help Groups

United Kingdom:

ALCOHOLICS ANONYMOUS: P.O. Box 1, Stonebow House, Stonebow, York, YO1 2NJ. Tel: 0904 644026

AL-ANON: 61 Great Dover Street, London SE1 4YF. Tel: 01 403 0888

ADULT CHILDREN OF ALCOHOLICS: 61 Great Dover Street, London SE1 4YF. Tel: 01 403 0888

ALATEEN: 61 Great Dover Street, London SE1 4YF. Tel: 01 403 0888

NARCOTICS ANONYMOUS: P.O. Box 704, London SW10 0RP. Tel: 01 352 8356

FAMILIES ANONYMOUS: 88 Caledonian Road, London N1 9DN. Tel: 01 731 8060

OVEREATERS ANONYMOUS: Tel: 01 868 4109

ANOREXICS ANONYMOUS: Tel: 01 748 3994

GAMBLERS ANONYMOUS: Tel: 01 352 3060

CODEPENDENTS ANONYMOUS: Tel: 01 267 8044

Ireland:

ALCOHOLICS ANONYMOUS: 109 South Circular Road, Dublin 8. Tel: Dublin 538998 or 774809/714050

AL-ANON – HEADQUARTERS: 61 Great Dover Street, London SE1 4YF. Tel: 01-403 0888

NARCOTICS ANONYMOUS: P.O. Box 1386, Sherriff Street, Dublin 1

FAMILIES ANONYMOUS: – HEADQUARTERS 88 Caledonian Road, London N1 9DN. Tel: 01 278 8805

Australia:

ALCOHOLICS ANONYMOUS: P.O. Box 5321, Sydney, N.S.W. 2001. Tel: 02 290 2210

AL-ANON FAMILY GROUPS: P.O. Box 1002H, Melbourne, Vic. 3001. Tel: 03 62 4933

NARCOTICS ANONYMOUS: P.O. Box 440, Leichandt, N.S.W. 2040. Tel: 02 810 2020

NAR-ANON (Equivalent of Families Anonymous): P.O. Box Q108, Qu. Victoria Bldg., Sydney, N.S.W. 2000. Tel: 02 300 9736

Canada:

ALCOHOLICS ANONYMOUS: Suite 6, 1581 Bank Street, Ottawa, Ont. K1H 7Z3. Tel: 613 523 9977

AL-ANON FAMILY GROUPS: P.O. Box 182, Madison Square Station, New York, NY10159. Tel: 212 683 1771

NARCOTICS ANONYMOUS: 161 Princess Street West, North Bay, Ont. P1B 6C5

FAMILIES ANONYMOUS HEADQUARTERS: P.O. Box 528, Van Nuys, CA 91408. Tel: 213 989 7841

New Zealand:

ALCOHOLICS ANONYMOUS: P.O. Box 6458, Wellington, N.I. Tel: 859 455
AL-ANON FAMILY GROUPS: Suite 4, Charter House, 56 Customs Street, Auckland. Tel: 794 871
NARCOTICS ANONYMOUS: P.O. Box 2858, Christchurch
FAMILIES ANONYMOUS: No known information. For up to date information, write to Families Anonymous, P.O. Box 528, Van Nuys, CA 91408, USA

South Africa:

ALCOHOLICS ANONYMOUS: P.O. Box 23005, Joubert Park 2044. Tel: 23 7219
AL-ANON FAMILY GROUPS: P.O. Box 2077, Johannesburg, Transvaal 2000. Tel: 011 29 6696
NARCOTICS ANONYMOUS: No known information at this time. The World Service Office may be able to help you. Their address is NA World Service Office, 16155 Wyndotte Street, Van Nuys, CA 91406, USA
FAMILIES ANONYMOUS: For up to date information contact Families Anonymous in USA

U.S.A.:

ALCOHOLICS ANONYMOUS: Box 459, Grand Central Station, New York, NY 17
AL-ANON FAMILY GROUPS INC.: P.O. Box 182, Madison Square Station, New York, NY 10
NARCOTICS ANONYMOUS: 16155 Wyndotte Street, Van Nuys, CA 91406. Tel: 818 780 3951
FAMILIES ANONYMOUS: P.O. Box 528, Van Nuys, CA 91480

Note: The telephone numbers and addresses given above tend to be of the headquarters in the different countries. For more localized telephone numbers, check the area telephone directory.

Other Helpful Agencies

AIDS HELPLINE, Terrence Higgins Trust: Tel: 01 833 2971
CHILDLINE (Sexual Abuse): Tel: 0800 1111
GAY SWITCHBOARD: Tel: 01 837 7234
GINGERBREAD (Self-help groups for one-parent families): Tel: 01 240 0953
INCEST CRISIS LINE: Tel: 01 890 4732
LESBIAN LINE: Tel: 01 251 6911
LONDON WOMENS AID (refuges): Tel: 01 251 6537/8
NATIONAL ASSOCIATION OF ONE PARENT FAMILIES: Tel: 01 267 1361
PARENTS ANONYMOUS (for parents who are worried that they may abuse their children: Tel: 01 263 8919
SAMARITANS: (see local telephone directory)
TRANX (help for those dependent on tranquillizers or sleeping pills): Tel: 01 427 2065